RESOLUTE

ALSO BY BENJAMIN HALL

Saved: A War Reporter's Mission to Make It Home

RESOLUTE

How We Humans Keep Finding Ways
to Beat the Toughest Odds

BENJAMIN
HALL

HARPER
INFLUENCE

HarperCollins books may be purchased for educational, business, or sales promotional use. For information, please email the Special Markets Department at SPsales@harpercollins.com.

FIRST EDITION

Library of Congress Cataloging-in-Publication Data has been applied for.

ISBN 978-0-06-339010-2

25 26 27 28 29 LBC 5 4 3 2 1

For all of you who've been knocked down—know you have the strength to get back up. And that you will be stronger every time you do.

And for all of you who help to lift up others—know that you make us all stronger. Never stop doing so.

CONTENTS

RESOLUTE

INTRODUCTION

Almost from the day they carried me out of the country, missing a leg, most of a foot, and part of a hand, I wanted to go back. Few people thought it was a good idea. Some tried to talk me out of it. The country was still at war. The capital was still the target of Russian cruise missiles. The village where I'd been injured no longer existed as a village but only as the ruins of a thousand cratered homes. And yet, in my mind, it was never a question of if, but when.

I had to go back.

And so, 614 days after a missile attack outside Kyiv nearly killed me, I did.

A few months earlier, I received an invitation to travel to Kyiv and interview Ukrainian president Volodymyr Zelenskyy in Mariinskyi Palace, from where he'd been conducting the battle to save his country from the militarily superior Russian forces that invaded on February 24, 2022. There was great news value to the interview, but for me there was something else.

The war in Ukraine has been one of the deadliest for journalists to cover: more than one hundred journalists or media workers have been the victims of violence in Ukraine since the 2022 invasion, and at least eighteen have been killed—an astonishing number that includes my great friend and colleague Pierre Zakrzewski, a veteran Fox News cameraman, and Oleksandra Kuvshynova, a twenty-four-year-old Ukrainian journalist who served as our fixer, both killed in the same attack that crippled me.

President Zelenskyy knew my story, and one of the reasons he invited me to return, I believe, was to demonstrate the resilience of journalists, who—like his country's courageous warriors and civilians—refused to be cowed by Russian aggression. In fact, journalists from all over the globe continue to pour into Ukraine, seeking the front lines, finding the story, doing their jobs.

For me, there was a personal element as well. My escape from Ukraine after the bombing had been improbable, all but doomed to fail, yet I'd somehow made it out alive and all the way back to my home in London, to my family. Returning to Ukraine was a chance to retake this most unlikely escape in reverse. To relive the many impossible events that had to happen for me to survive, only this time with a clearer head and a more functional body. A chance to appreciate and be thankful for all the twists of fate and acts of heroism that brought me home. It was important for me to confront anew everything that had happened, rather than look away and leave it in the past. Like I said, I am a journalist, and a journalist can't look away.

There was more to my story that needed to be told.

So it was that I arranged a meeting with a doctor from the Military Clinical Hospital in Kyiv, Ukraine's capital—the brave Ukrainian doctor who, in between shifts as an armed sentry for the national army, saved my life after the bombing.

It was in that hospital in March 2022 that my team of rescuers dispatched from abroad by Save Our Allies found me in a bed, metal rods sticking out of my left thigh, a drain tube attached to my skull, a cigarette lighter–sized piece of shrapnel lodged in my throat, parts of my left eye missing, my right leg amputated at the knee, and deep burns across much of my body. The Ukrainian doctor was dead set against moving me, afraid that any passage on the country's gutted, bomb-shelled streets might dislodge the shrapnel in my throat and kill me—one of several ways that leaving the hospital might have cost me my life.

Finally, he did agree to let me leave, patched up and hammered together just enough to make the trip feasible. And now, on my unlikely return to see him almost two years later, there he was again, waiting to greet me along with a handful of nurses who'd helped keep me alive.

I did not recognize the doctor—I had been close to death when we first met.

But he recognized me.

When he saw me, his eyes widened and his face went white, and he began to cry. He walked up to me and looked hard at my face, as if I weren't real.

As if he were looking at a ghost.

"You were gone," he said. "My God, you were *gone*. You shouldn't be here. It is a miracle you are here."

I hugged him and I told him I agreed with him. I *was* gone, a bloody mess, clinging to a heartbeat, and yet there I was, 614 days later, walking upright on a prosthetic leg, my facial scars nearly invisible, looking from the outside like the healthiest person alive. I'd been at the very brink of extinction, but something had pulled me back.

This book is about that something.

* * *

For most of my adult life I've been a journalist—specifically, a war correspondent. I've covered bombings and battles, witnessed heroism and atrocities, seen brutal death and unbearable injury up close, and along the way I have often wondered one thing:

How would I react if I was the guy on the stretcher?

Now I know.

I told the story of the bomb attack and the start of my recovery in my first book, *Saved: A War Reporter's Mission to Make It Home.* Yet as soon as I finished that book, I knew there was more to my experience I wanted to share. As a journalist, I'd begun reporting my own story in the minutes after I awakened on that asphalt slope in Horenka. The first thing I tried to do after regaining consciousness was take out my cell phone and snap pictures of my missing leg and mangled foot. My impulse, even before any primal survival instinct kicked in, was to document what was happening to me. *To get the story.* I never stopped doing that all through my recovery and the process of writing my first book. And I'm not quite done yet.

In a way, it's the same story I've been chasing throughout my fifteen years as a war correspondent. I've searched for it in the hills of Aleppo and the rubble of Mosul, the valleys of Kabul and the carnage in Mogadishu—places where civilization had all but collapsed and human beings were at their most vulnerable. I understood it was a thing that existed in the extremes of life and often on the edges of death. I'd caught glimpses of it, and I'd wondered if it was possible to understand it without experiencing it.

What I was chasing, the story I wanted to tell, was the story of humanity's profound and powerful will to survive.

The way we humans keep finding ways to beat the toughest odds.

Before the bombing, I believed it was something I could write about after just having witnessed it from a distance.

But it was only after I was nearly killed in Horenka, when I found myself in a fierce struggle to live and recover, that I truly understood what it was that had so intrigued me.

You see, most of us will never be challenged in the way that people caught up in wars are challenged.

But every one of us *will* be challenged in some significant way, or in many ways. We will all face long odds at some point, and we will all confront some obstacle that at first seems insurmountable. Life, in a way, is a series of such tests—of character, of will, of resolve.

What intrigues me is how we keep managing to pass these tests, sometimes after believing we are doomed to fail.

Humans are, I have learned, incredibly resilient creatures. We are capable of summoning a mysterious extra gear from deep within that can rescue us from terrible predicaments and propel us to wondrous new heights.

We are, in a word, *resolute.*

In fact, resilience is one of our most primal imperatives as human beings. "The human instinct to survive is our most powerful drive," a recent study in *Psychology Today* declared. "Since animals climbed out of the primordial muck and as our ancestors rose from all fours to walk upright, evolution has been guided by its ability to help us survive and reproduce. Just about everything humans have become serves that purpose."

Or to borrow a phrase from the evolutionary biologist Richard Dawkins, the human animal is "a survival machine."

This book is a result of the hardest journalistic mission I've ever undertaken—an inquisition into why I'm still alive.

It's both a continuation of my physical, mental, and spiritual ordeal and an exploration of how that ordeal, though unique to me in its details, is, at its essence, universal. Because the challenges I have faced are the same kinds of challenges we are *all* capable of overcoming—challenges most of us confront many times in our lives. So instead of looking at geopolitics and war strategies, I'll be tunneling into the human psyche in search of its secrets and truths.

In *Resolute*, I share my own experiences—on battlefields, in war-torn Kyiv, in hospitals, and at home with my wife and daughters—as well as the experiences and insight of several remarkable people I've met in the course of my continuing recovery, including other people who have confronted their own mortality, or helped someone who has.

What these people share with me is the experience of dealing with a truly dire situation—and the knowledge that these situations can push us to tap into new levels of tenacity, potency, and resolve. The message all these people conveyed is simple and direct: the capacity to not only survive adversity but to use it to become better, more evolved, and more compassionate human beings is something *that resides in us all*.

I will also take a closer look at certain events that happened between the bombing and my return to London six months later. As a journalist, I wanted to drill down deeper on these moments and, with the benefit of time and distance, mine them for more meaning and insight and, hopefully, a little extra wisdom along the way.

You should know that I've always been an optimist. Even after the bombing, a doctor told me I was suffering from post-traumatic optimism. When I talk to people about everything I went through, they sometimes marvel at how I've maintained such a positive attitude.

"Whatever it is that you have," they say, "can you bottle it and give it to me?"

This book is the best I can do.

I'm certainly not an expert in anything. I don't have advanced degrees. I cannot write a guidebook or handbook filled with lessons and exercises. All I can do is what I do for a living—tell a story. Yet I hope that what I have gone through in the last two years will resonate in some way with you, and with whatever challenges you face in your own lives—physical, financial, emotional, aspirational.

I also hope that the things I discovered about myself will inspire you to believe in your own remarkable power to take on any challenge and beat the toughest odds.

1

RECKONING

March 2022

BROOKE ARMY MEDICAL CENTER

Fort Sam Houston, Texas

Twenty-four sleepless, hallucinatory hours in the frigid belly of a C-17 military freight plane were, mercifully, over. Now I was in a Type 3 MICU ambulance speeding down Interstate 35 South in San Antonio. It was 2 a.m. and the traffic was light; I was alert, exhausted, and in pain. We took Exit 162 and pulled through the George C. Beach Avenue entrance and into the sprawling Brooke Army Medical Center complex.

This was the place where people like me—the lucky ones—came to face our fates.

I was wheeled through the Trauma Center straight to the Surgical Research Burn Center. Of all my multiple injuries, the burns across my back and legs were deemed the most urgent. Nurses and techs gave me a Trauma Care Primary Survey—a quick check of my airway, breathing, circulation, and neurological status—before surveying my burns. Then I was rushed to an operating room and swung onto a table beneath two eerily bright, tire-sized LED surgical lights. At least ten medical professionals swarmed me and got straight to it. All that time at high elevation on the cavernous C-17 Globemaster had worsened my condition, as expected—decreased blood pressure, high fevers, delirium. That pointed to dangerous bacteria in my system. A serious hidden infection, the doctors knew, could be fatal.

Which meant I would have to be taken apart.

Bit by bit, the unraveling proceeded. First the gown, then the dirtied bandages. I lay naked on the table as doctors probed every open wound—the stump of my right knee, the hole through my left foot, deep gashes in my left hand—looking for signs of infection. Even wounds that were stitched up and sealed were unstitched and pulled apart. All was laid bare. Different doctors peered into my tattered body—ophthalmological surgeons, brain surgeons, burn specialists, neurological experts—as is common with polytrauma stemming from blast injuries. The damage is extensive. The blasts affect multiple systems. They ravage your resources. My doctors needed to quickly determine:

This is what it looks like. This is the lay of the land. This is where we are right now with the patient, Benjamin Hall.

They needed to know just what was left of me.

*   *   *

By then I fully understood that my life as I knew it ended on March 14, 2022, in the deserted village of Horenka, Ukraine, on the outskirts of Kyiv.

I was there with a crew from Fox News, where I worked as the

U.S. State Department correspondent. The crew included my friend Pierre Zakrzewski, fifty-five, and Oleksandra "Sasha" Kuvshynova, our gutsy twenty-four-year-old fixer and translator. We were there to cover Russia's invasion of the country, which began eighteen days earlier. On March 14, two Ukrainian soldiers escorted our crew to Horenka, where we filmed the total devastation of the village and spoke with a troop of defiant Ukrainian soldiers.

We were done reporting for the day and were driving out of the village and back to Kyiv when it happened.

An unknown Russian craft fired three missiles at us and blew up our small red car just before we steered out of the town. I was in the back seat, sandwiched between Pierre and Sasha, while the two Ukrainian soldiers were in front. The first missile struck thirty feet in front of us. The second landed next to the car, plunging me into a darkness that felt like death. That is when a true miracle happened. Out of the blackness came a vision and a voice, thin but distinct, imploring me to get out of the car. It was my beautiful six-year-old daughter, Honor, whom I'd left back home in London with her two young sisters, Iris and Hero, and her mother, my wife, Alicia. Over and over Honor was saying, *Daddy, you've got to get out of the car*. I listened and I *did* get out of the burning car, and took one or two steps before a third missile exploded next to us and threw me back into blackness. When I awakened, I was flat on the asphalt ground, not far from the smoldering skeleton of what used to be our car. I was bleeding badly and missing the bottom half of my right leg, and much of my left foot. I was also on fire.

The miracle continued. A series of improbable events unfolded that allowed me to survive the blasts that killed both Pierre and Sasha, as well as the two brave Ukraine soldiers who were driving us, Mykola Kravchenko and Serhiy Mashovets. I had been in the death seat, the only spot in the red car with no quick exit, yet I was the only one of the five of us to make it out alive. Surviving the blast, however, was just the beginning of my ordeal. After I was rescued, I needed to get out of Ukraine and to the safety of an American military base, which meant traveling hundreds of miles west to Poland without jarring the hunk of shrapnel lodged in my throat, or worsening any of my other severe injuries to the point where I would bleed out, all while a countrywide shoot-to-kill curfew had just been imposed.

Somehow, all these unlikely pieces fell into place and I was delivered to Landstuhl Regional Medical Center, near the United States' Ramstein Air Base in Germany, and from there to the brilliant surgeons and nurses at Brooke Army Medical Center (BAMC) at Fort Sam Houston in Texas—the beginning of my long journey back to recovery.

Now I was in an operating room at BAMC, being dissected like a specimen, and I understood I'd entered a new phase of my journey. First, I had survived the blasts. Then I'd made it out of Ukraine. For ten days at Landstuhl I was treated as an emergency case, monitored and restored to a functional baseline of health. Now, at BAMC, it was time for the accounting. The reckoning. Judgment Day. I had survived, and that was a blessing. But what next? What came now? What, exactly, would the rest of my life look like?

Eventually a doctor came into my room in the intensive care unit and read me the laundry list of the injuries I'd sustained. I already knew the basics: one leg was gone from the knee down, the other foot was a mess, and my left hand and eye were in bad shape. What I still needed to know was, what would I get to keep? Would I need another amputation, maybe two? Would I lose my eye? What other potentially devastating internal injuries did I not know about? I've never been afraid to receive bad news, and I wasn't afraid when the doctor came into my room, his face at best serious, at worst grim. But I did feel my muscles tense and my nerves fire warning signals to the rest of me. The verdict was in, and I was about to hear it.

"Let's go from top to bottom," the doctor said, before reciting a litany of bodily destruction. A depressed skull fracture, or a hole in my skull, that caused a traumatic brain injury but did not necessitate immediate neurosurgery; a retinal detachment in my left eye, as well as the loss of my iris, lens, and cornea—the result of shrapnel spattering my face; a shattered metacarpal bone in my left thumb and extensive damage to my left hand, the skin torn away and the tendons on the back of my thumb exposed; my right leg amputated just below the knee; my left leg missing a fair amount of calf muscle and all the tendons that powered the foot, which, due to its condition, might have to be amputated as well. And, of course, significant burns from the top of my left leg to the bottom, and on my left hand, back, and buttocks, all requiring multiple delicate and painful skin grafts over the course of the next several months.

What's more, at every step I would be at risk of potentially fatal infections.

In those first few days at BAMC, I was told I could expect to remain at the medical center in Texas for at least the next two years.

There it was—the reckoning. The moment when my journey changed from a battle of survival to a battle of will.

No matter what, I would need enormous amounts of help from literally dozens of people, and without them I had no chance of any meaningful recovery. There were also a million variables, meaning luck and grace would surely play a huge part in my rehabilitation.

But the most critical work, the day-to-day dogfight for incremental progress, the mental and physical overhaul needed to confront the challenge, would be mine and mine alone.

The first question I had to ask myself, then, once I fully accepted my situation, was whether I believed I had it in me to not only face this challenge but to fight my way through it, and *keep* fighting through it, no matter how hard or impossible things got.

In other words—*was I made of strong enough stuff?*

Here I was able to apply a lesson I'd learned in covering the many wars and conflicts and disasters during the last fifteen years—a lesson I would keep learning and relearning over the long course of my recovery and rehab.

What I learned is that the trait that most shapes the destinies of people and nations and movements, more critical even than bravery and cunning and all the other human traits, is *the capacity to withstand and recover from adversity.*

Or, in a word, *resilience.*

"Campaigns and battles are nothing but a long series of difficulties to be overcome," U.S. five-star general George C. Marshall, commander of Allied operations in the Pacific and Europe in World War II, memorably said. "The lack of equipment, the lack of food, the lack of this or that are only excuses; the real leader displays his quality in his triumphs over adversity, however great it may be."

It is a thought echoed by any number of war historians and participants. "Resiliency does not guarantee victory," Regents professor James L. Regens once said. "But history is littered with examples where the absence of resiliency ended in defeat."

Resilience is our genetic inheritance; it's what we're wired to exhibit. It is not something we even have to think about; it is just there, built in, ready to go. The human animal is not born to quit or surrender; we are born to endure, to keep going, to push further, to explore deeper, to be strong and determined—to be resolute. This is simply how we are designed. We are built to rise to the moment.

Resilience is our default setting.

So when my primary surgeon, Colonel Joe Alderete, told me I would likely be stuck in the hospital in Texas for two years before I could properly walk out on my own and be with my beloved family in London, I knew instantly that this would not be my fate.

"To be honest," I told Dr. Alderete, "I was hoping it might be less time than that."

In fact, my goal was to make it home in time for my fortieth birthday on July 23, which would mean my stay at BAMC was not two years but rather closer to just *six months*.

This was not false bravado or wishful thinking. This was my natural, inherent resilience immediately kicking into gear. I believed what I said, and I believed, without even thinking about it, that I could do it.

How could I be so confident?

I was sure because I've witnessed resilience all over the world, and I've seen what people facing colossal adversity are capable of. Adversity much greater than what I was facing. Knowing this, all I had to do was learn how to *trust* that I had it in me to fight back and fight hard, because that's just what we humans do.

We fight back, and we fight hard.

To anyone facing a fearsome challenge they aren't sure they can overcome, I would say: *Trust that you have what it takes to battle against any adversity. Trust that the power of resilience is already inside you, waiting to be deployed.*

2

THE OLIVE TREE

August 2022

London, England

I dug the shovel in the ground and pulled up enough dirt to plant a tree. An olive tree, only six feet tall now, but one day likely to grow to twenty feet, with silvery leaves and fragrant white flowers and a thick, gnarled trunk. One of the world's oldest cultivated trees, it might live for hundreds of years, maybe even thousands. The root ball planted in our front yard was meant to grow alongside us—me, my wife, Alicia, and our children.

Alicia and I had just bought the home together in 2015, in the same month our first daughter, Honor, was born. It was a nineteenth-century terrace-style house in the middle of London, and one of the reasons we bought it was that it had plenty of room for more children. Sure enough, Alicia and I had two more daughters, Iris and Hero, and we added a big chocolate Labrador, Bosco, and the five of us were truly, spectacularly happy in that old house. It felt like it might even be our forever home. By the time I left on assignment for Ukraine in 2022, the olive tree out front was tall and strapping and, it seemed, permanent. Something that would just always be there.

Then the bombing happened, and I spent six months recovering from my injuries at Brooke Army Medical Center in Texas, away from Alicia and our daughters in London. In that time, I did a lot of thinking. Primarily I thought about my family, and all the things we would do together once I was home. I thought about the simplest joys of our lives—Sunday mornings in bed with the girls, afternoons in the park with Bosco, little moments here and there. I thought about our home, and I thought about our olive tree. These things that mattered to me.

When you're struck by a catastrophe of any kind, and your life is upended, you must decide what it is that matters *most* to you and use that as motivation to never give up. You must ask yourself, *What is the thing that inspires me to fight the hardest not to lose?*

For me, the answer was clear. It was the voice of my daughter—all my daughters, really—that brought me back from the brink of death. And it was Alicia and my daughters who inspired me every day at BAMC to fight as hard as I possibly could not to lose what we had. I wanted to heal as quickly as I could so I could get back to London and be with my family and pick up where we left off.

When I finally did leave BAMC in late summer of 2022 and land back in London, Alicia ran onto the plane and hugged me in my seat before I even had a chance to get up. It was the most meaningful hug of my life. It meant I had made it. I had survived. I was back. Alicia was there to handle the last leg of my long, painful journey to reunion, and the sight of her kind, smiling, beaming face aboard the plane—something I'd been envisioning for weeks—was overwhelming. I could hardly wade through my profound feelings of relief and joy and gratitude and muster a coherent thought, beyond, *I'm home again. I'm home again. I'm home again.*

*   *   *

Heading back to London I was determined to make my return as undramatic as possible. I didn't want everything to have to swirl around me and my needs. Nor did I want to disrupt the lives of Alicia and the girls. They had soldiered on without me for months, and they had developed a rhythm; the last thing I ever wished to do was barrel through the door and drastically alter the system they had created. I wanted to calmly slide in and pick up where we'd left off, no fuss, no hassle, just—*normalcy.*

But that became one of the earliest lessons I learned along my journey—*there was no normal anymore.*

The most obvious and immediate obstacle to just picking up where I left off was the house we loved so much—it was simply not suitable for our new situation. Beyond the narrow turning spaces and sharp angles, there were stairs—three flights of them, each one a steep twenty steps. The prosthetics on both my legs were new to me, and though I'd practiced taking steps while at BAMC, a climb of twenty stairs was not something I could comfortably do. What's more, since my legs were the most problematic and painful area for me, and I was sometimes "off my legs"—unstrapped from my prosthetic right leg and prosthetic left foot and leg brace—getting around the house would be a real challenge. For instance, the only way I could get up the stairs from the first floor to the second was by hoisting myself up step by step on my bottom, using my hands to propel me upward. I dreaded having to do this in front of my family, and having the girls see me in such a vulnerable way, but I should have known our cheerful daughters would make a game out of it and try to beat me upstairs, scooching step by step just like me. They won almost every time, but God bless them for turning an unpleasant task into a silly, beautiful ritual.

Early on, we had a visit from a consultant named Phill Gill, who is an expert at helping people with disabilities reenter and adapt to their homes. Phill was one of the many remarkable professionals Fox News arranged for me to ease my transition back home—and an example of the level of care I was blessed to receive, and that most people, I fully realized, don't have access to. Phill appraised every nook and cranny in the house and advised us to make several adjustments. But as he sat with us at the kitchen table, he also shared a bit of wisdom that struck a chord with us.

"You have to be able to make it a home, not just a place you live," he said. "You need to make everything feel like a regular activity and not a difficult challenge. You don't want to feel disabled in your own home. The house has to work for *you*. And to be honest, this house doesn't."

By then, Alicia and I already knew that. Phill had dropped in to see Alicia fully two months before I made it home, to begin to prepare her for what would need to happen. After assessing the house for the first time, he called Alicia with a warning.

"Look, I don't want to worry you," he told her, "but I am really worried."

Our house, as he would stress again two months later, just wasn't the right place for me. Yes, we could make it work somehow, but that would involve quite a bit of disruption. After Phill told us that our house did not work for us, Alicia and I sat back down in the kitchen to discuss our options. "One of my worries in the last few weeks before you came back," Alicia candidly told me, "was that we'd have to transform the house into a kind of rehab center." She envisioned a place with ramps and pulleys and bars and carers everywhere—a house built around me and my needs, rather than a home for us all.

Now, Alicia had always been willing to make any compromise necessary, and she was ready to make even more compromises to make things work for us. There was nothing she wouldn't sacrifice to the cause of reintegrating me into our life together, something she proved over and over in the weeks and months that followed. But as we sat at the kitchen table laying out our future, I told her that her fear that our home would turn into a hospital was exactly *my* fear as well. It was the last thing I would want to see happen. I had vowed to be the least disruptive presence I could be upon my return, and after the visit from Phill Gill both Alicia and I knew what that meant.

"We're going to have to move," Alicia said.

We told the girls about moving and they were just fine with packing up. We were determined to find a new home that wouldn't require the girls to change schools or lose friends or anything like that, so switching homes just felt like another adventure for them. Phill helped us look at a few new houses and we quickly found one that was perfect. There were only two stairways, and neither was steep or long. And there was plenty of room on the ground floor to add what we needed. But when Alicia asked about renting it, she was told it was no longer on the market. Alicia, being Alicia, chose not to accept that answer. She kept calling and inquiring and somehow persuaded them to rent us the house. I'm not sure how she did it, but I'm not at all surprised that she did.

Phill came in to look over our new place, and we agreed to add an open shower room (with a bench in it) and a secondary bedroom on the ground floor, for the operations I still had ahead that would leave me unable to get upstairs, where Alicia and I would normally sleep. The new house would be much easier for me to get around in a wheelchair, which meant it would make life easier for all of us.

Changing homes was an acknowledgment that we would never be returning to what had been our normal lives. That's because there *was* no normal anymore.

It's human nature for anyone facing a major challenge in life to wish that things would simply return to the way they were before. When I was at BAMC, I yearned for the simplest pleasures of my former life. I dreamed of roaming with Bosco along the tracks of Holland Park. I yearned to get back to the gloriously uncomplicated and joyful routine Alicia and I and our family had fashioned.

But deep down I already knew I would never truly be able to go back to what was normal before. I suppose I knew that the instant I first realized in Horenka that much of my right leg was missing. Things were going to be different because *I* was going to be different. Normal, for us, would be whatever our new lives wound up looking like.

What I learned from having to walk away from the old house Alicia and I both loved was this:

We need to be clear-eyed about the reality of our situation.

As a journalist, I have always tried to see things as they are. To not look away. Pretending things are different or deluding myself about what I was up against wouldn't help anyone. For me, the clear-eyed reality was that returning to "normal" simply wasn't possible. Hanging on to the goal of recapturing my old life would have been a waste of time.

Of course, some of us may face challenges that, once surmounted, allow for a return to the way things were. And perhaps returning to normal—resuming a job, having a beer with friends, talking a walk in the park—is all the motivation you will ever need. But in my case, Alicia and I accepted that when I returned to London, we would be starting a completely *new* life together. When I was at BAMC and Alicia and I jumped on FaceTime to talk—but only after the girls had their turns first and eventually drifted back to whatever they were doing before the call—Alicia and I never talked about trying to get back to our old lives. We knew that wouldn't happen. Everything we discussed was about the future, not the past, with the understanding that we were going to have to adapt and be flexible and go wherever our new lives took us. And this turned out to be extremely liberating. We didn't have time to dwell on what we had lost or what we could no longer do. Instead, we embraced the challenge of creating a *new* life as a family.

I was lucky in that this approach fit well with my instinct to always be moving forward. As Alicia puts it, "You have itchy feet." Even before the bombing I never wanted to do the same things over and over. I enjoyed going from assignment to assignment, soaking up new experiences, getting to view things from different angles. I never wanted a "normal" life, and I still believe it's a mistake to choose "normal" as a goal. To me, it just isn't a big enough goal. It was limiting and it likely wouldn't provide me with enough motivation. I needed bigger dreams and aspirations, mainly because I was facing the kind of adversity that was going to be life-changing no matter what I decided to do. Clinging to small goals, I believed, could only hold me back and slow my progress.

Confronting challenges, especially seemingly impossible ones, changes us. I know they have always changed me. Surviving close calls in Misrata and Mogadishu transformed the way I perceived the world, as well as how much I was willing to risk to go out and report on that world. The changes weren't massive and maybe not even perceptible to most, but I knew I was different because of what I had been through. In many ways, I was a better person because of the things I'd experienced.

This was one of the most essential lessons for me to learn in my journey of recovery: *accept that things will be different and aspire to build the best new life you can.*

* * *

Understanding this, and actually doing it, are two different things. Saying goodbye to normal isn't easy. In fact, it can be quite hard. I've never been the type to dwell on what I've lost or what has changed. As a journalist, I couldn't afford to be. I had to quickly accept and adapt to whatever my new reality was. But as forward-thinking as I tried to always be, there were many times when I missed certain things that had been lost to me.

Not long ago, I drove past our former London home just to get a look at the old place. I stood outside on the sidewalk and looked in the front yard for the olive tree I had planted nearly a decade before. There it was, in its prominent place, taller, sturdier, even more permanent. Its trunk was thicker and gnarlier, as promised, giving it a sort of ancient air. I thought back to the day when it first went into the earth—the day Alicia and I literally planted roots.

But something was different. The tree didn't look the same. Olive trees require a good deal of care and clipping and pruning to keep them healthy and help them spread and grow, and it was immediately clear the new owners of the house weren't as attentive to the tree as Alicia and I had been. They had, in fact, let it grow wild. It was a bit of a sad sight for me, and I took a moment to mourn what the tree had once represented for us.

Yet not everything from my old life that I reexperienced was a disappointment. Far from it. After many, many months of hard work and setbacks and triumphs, I was finally strong enough to hit a major milestone: walking our chocolate lab Bosco again. When the day finally came, I drove Bosco to the park and the two of us slowly made our way around, both of us thrilled to be picking up where we'd left off. Bosco didn't see anything different about me at all. To him, I was the same Benji I'd always been.

It just so happened that Bosco had recently developed a large cyst on his right leg that couldn't be operated on, and as a result he had to hobble around just like me. There we were, the two of us, limping around on wounded legs rather than sprinting the way we used to when we were younger and healthier. But the pace of our walk didn't matter in the least. Our morning together went on as it usually did, with us reveling in the sensory pleasures of being outdoors and, most of all, being in each other's presence.

Just like normal.

3

GLASS HOUSES

September 2022

West London, London

People who live in glass houses shouldn't throw stones.

I was sitting in our living room less than two months after getting home to London, across from my occupational therapist, a psychologist who specializes in treating patients with traumatic brain injury (TBI). We met regularly once a week, one of six or seven weekly appointments I had to keep in those early months. The girls were at school and the house was quiet. The therapist flipped through flash cards and asked me a series of what I perceived to be softball questions. At one point, she read out the "glass houses" proverb, the one we've all heard a million times, and asked, "Can you explain what this means?"

I started to answer but no words came out. I tried again but still, nothing. No collection of thoughts formed in my brain into anything like a response. I sat in the living room in silence, on the verge of an answer but never quite there, and I was surprised to see that suddenly I was crying.

Because I hadn't merely been asked a question.

This was a *test*.

On top of the physical injuries caused by the missile attack, I was also diagnosed with a TBI. The extent of any brain damage I'd suffered was initially unknown, beyond the fact that in the hospital at BAMC I seemed alert and lucid and quite capable of forming sentences.

During my months of recovery at BAMC, a series of exams and therapy sessions revealed that my TBI *did* have a perceptible effect on my ability to comprehend and communicate certain things. Of all the harsh truths I had to absorb in the aftermath of the bombing—including the realization I would never walk again without prosthetics—it was the impact of the bombing on my brain that hit me the hardest. The idea I might not be able to mentally function at the same level I had before the attack was terrifying.

The job of a journalist, by its nature, demands quick thinking. Covering wars and conflicts is all about reacting to sudden, unexpected happenings that, if not handled properly, could cost you your life. Out in the field I had to be able to instantly assess situations, weigh risks, determine allies and enemies, scan for escape routes, and then, in the same split second, form a decision on how to react and commit entirely to it. The slightest gap in this synaptic process could mean the difference between life and death.

Now, after the bombing, there was a gap.

Of course, I had been extremely lucky. Whatever the extent of the damage to my brain, I was still able to make jokes and tell stories and interact with my doctors and nurses at BAMC, and with Alicia and our daughters back in London. I could still summon memories from long ago and make detailed plans. My knowledge of history and geo-politics was mostly there, as was my insight into current events. My personality, it seemed to me, hadn't changed much at all.

I was, as far as most people could tell, still Ben Hall.

And yet—I knew something had changed.

* * *

Shortly after I left BAMC and returned to London, Alicia and I agreed to join her friend Eugenie for lunch and to watch the funeral of Queen Elizabeth II at her house. It was our first outing with friends since before I went to Kyiv, and I was both excited and nervous about it. The seven or eight people there were all people I knew, and I was sure they'd go out of their way to make things welcoming for me. But I didn't know how I would react to being around so many people in a social situation again. At Eugenie's house we took our seats at a long table, and lunch was served. The main topic of conversation was the queen.

I was relieved to be part of a discussion that wasn't about me. For months, nearly the full focus of my life had been on the granular de-tails of my injuries and rehab, and most discussions I had, from casual ones to conference calls with professionals, were centered entirely on my condition. But on the day of the queen's funeral, after a few in-quiries about how I was doing, I ceased to be the main event, which was a huge relief.

Then a friend turned the discussion to Prince Charles, now the king, and how his life would now change, and everyone chimed in with jokes and opinions, and I realized I was having trouble keeping up with all the banter.

It was all too quick for me. I couldn't form thoughts and replies fast enough to keep up the conversation. I heard what everyone was saying, and I understood it, but it was all scrolling past me far too speedily. Instead of joining in, as I normally would have, I silently slipped out of the conversation, incapable of catching up. In years past I'd had a million tableside conversations about anything and everything and I'd enjoyed the lively back-and-forth, the lightning flashes of wit and insight. But on that day, I was lost. I had nothing to contribute. I froze mute in my seat.

I'm not sure anyone noticed how hard a time I was having, other than Alicia. She could tell I was struggling and frustrated. This quiet, removed person most certainly *wasn't* the Benji she knew. Protective as always, Alicia arranged for us to discreetly leave the get-together right after the meal finished—much earlier than we would have in the old days.

The lunch was a cold dose of reality. For me, it was the realization that I'd been living in a bubble for several months, a bubble in which no one even *knew* the old Ben Hall and thus had no expectations. But as soon as I was back in the real world, among friends and family, the gap between who I'd been and who I was became more glaring. Discovering that simple banter was beyond my capability was crushing. A shattered bone could heal or be fixed. But a shattered brain?

Alicia too experienced an unwelcome awakening at our friend's house. By then she had already accepted that many things about her life would have to change, and she was sanguine about the sacrifices she would have to make. But she hadn't considered the possibility that she might have to continually watch over me and help me get through basic human exchanges. At our friend's house she kept a steady eye on me and wondered if and when she might need to step in. Would I have to be helped upstairs to the bathroom? Did I need to be bailed out of a conversation? Just how much care and scrutiny *was* I going to require?

"Well," Alicia gently told me on the drive home about watching me struggle, "I guess this is how our life might have to be."

* * *

Not too long after that lunch, I was sitting across from my occupational therapist for our weekly meeting, fighting tears as I struggled to explain the meaning behind the familiar proverb about glass houses.

I fumbled and grasped and could not summon a single word. It felt like being in quicksand and reaching for something to hold on to and only grabbing more sand. In the end I just gave up.

"I know it, I know it, I really do," I pleaded. "I just can't remember it."

I can count on one hand the number of times I've cried since the bombing: The miserable twenty-four hours I spent on a C-17 cargo plane. Seeing Alicia's beautiful face again in London. Feeling my three daughters climb all over me when we were reunited. I can think of many more times when I *should* have cried but didn't. I'm not much of a crier, and I never have been.

But on the day of that session, the fear and frustration got the best of me.

The TBI specialist settled me down.

"It's okay that you don't know," she said calmly. "People recover at different speeds. You just have to find a better method to summon the things in your mind that you know. You'll have to think about things a little bit differently."

I immediately knew what she was telling me. *That much*, I understood. I was facing a serious challenge. Things were going to be different. I had to find a way to *adapt*.

*   *   *

Resilience and the ability to adapt are intrinsically tied—as I was to discover, you can't have one without the other. The American Psychological Association defines *resilience* as "the process and outcome of successfully adapting to difficult or challenging life experiences, especially through mental, emotional, and behavioral flexibility and adjustment to external and internal demands."

The ability to adapt to new circumstances is one of our inheritances as human beings. According to Charles Darwin, adaptability is one of the crucial "useful" traits that evolution selects to perpetuate a species. One well-known paraphrase of Darwin's evolutionary theories suggests that it's not the strongest of the species that survives, nor the most intelligent, but rather the one that is most adaptable to change.

Or, to put it more starkly—*adapt or die.*

Adapting, essentially, is changing. As the environment around us changes, so must we. A new situation, a new challenge, requires a new approach. Whatever it was that worked for us before in overcoming adversity might not be enough to confront some new and different challenge. What I've learned over the last two years is that, while adaptability is instinctive, we are also capable of improving and honing our ability to adapt.

The APA also noted that "psychological research demonstrates the resources and skills associated with more positive adaptation (i.e., greater resilience) can be cultivated and practiced."

In other words, *we can all rebuild ourselves* into human beings who view and engage with the world differently in changing situations, access social resources more efficiently, and devise more powerful coping strategies.

Part of it is our mental approach to challenges. Do we survey a situation that may seem utterly dire and say, "There's no way I can overcome this"? Or do we say, "This is going to be hard but doable"? One approach likely sets us up for failure. The other frees us up to take bold action. The gulf between these two approaches is vast, yet it boils down to an adjustment of just two letters—can we make ourselves believe that something is possible rather than *im*possible, no matter how insurmountable the challenge may seem?

After the third missile landed near me in Horenka in 2022, I found myself in an all-but-impossible situation. I was critically injured, bleeding, and on fire, and could no longer use my legs. I was in an abandoned village and could not expect anyone to happen upon me by chance. There was no way to make a phone call or otherwise signal for help. The most probable outcome was bleeding to death on the asphalt or being captured by Russian soldiers, and likely meeting the same fate. The word that comes to mind is *doomed*.

Even after the miracle of a car driving by and its driver happening to see me waving from below the road, my situation improved, but only marginally. After my right leg was amputated below the knee, it was clear I would need extensive and specialized medical care that the small hospital in Kyiv could not hope to provide. Even if there was somewhere I could be taken, there was no one to take me and very little chance I'd get there, given that Kyiv had that very day been placed on a shoot-on-sight curfew.

As someone familiar with the situation put it, "the options available for an injured person's extraction out of Kyiv and to the border were severely limited to *nonexistent*."

Still—

—not once at any point in this span of thirty or so hours did I stop believing I'd make it home alive. How I'd survive, I didn't know. But

I just didn't believe I was doomed. I knew I could make it happen somehow. I knew there was a way.

Sure enough, an incredible sequence of events unfolded, defying all reason, and a way out for me *was* found. Was it sheer luck? Or divine intervention? It would take me some time to reflect on that unlikely moment and come to some conclusion about it (something I describe in a later chapter). But that day, all I knew was that a team of seasoned extraction specialists—former military, medical, and intelligence professionals assembled and deployed in secret for just such missions, assembled by the remarkable Sarah Verardo and her amazing organization Save Our Allies, and assigned to rescue me by Fox News—somehow managed to make it past dozens of dangerous roadblocks and get into Kyiv, a city under siege. They then somehow managed to find me in a local hospital. Then, when they were advised that moving me at all would likely mean killing me because of the likelihood of Russian attacks and the terrible condition of the roads, the specialists refused to accept this as true and found a way to get me out of Ukraine via a secret government train to which civilians had no access or hope of ever getting aboard.

Because of these miracle workers, and against the greatest possible odds, I made it home to my family.

Even though I was completely aware of how utterly dire the situation was, I still never once believed I was going to die. This was the result of a simple calculus on my part—believing I was in an impossible situation *would not have helped me get out of it*.

I did not come by this conviction out of instinct or by default. Although my brain was scrambled by the trauma I'd endured and the intense pain I was feeling, I distinctly remember thinking at the time about what my role would be in the extraction, and how best I could help the mission succeed.

I realized I could be most useful by staying alert, ignoring my pain, going along with whatever plan was concocted, and above all staying positive. I could not be a drain on the operation; I could not draw attention away from the extraction by pulling it toward me. I had to be a silent but active participant in the events of that night, and I had to quickly adapt to whatever situation I found myself in.

To get to such a state of readiness, I made a mental adjustment. I worked deliberately to narrow my field of thought and vision to one simple, irreducible goal: get back to my family. Nothing else mattered. All else was a distraction to be ignored. Everything I did, everything I thought about, *had* to be in the service of achieving my one, singular goal. I had to shrink the world around me into a tiny thimble of hope.

I can tell you from experience that there is great power in isolating your focus. Refusing to dwell on the long odds against me and forcing myself to focus completely on the end goal of our mission—to get me back to my family—prevented me from slipping into a state of desperation or ever feeling that the actions we were taking were futile. That made it easier for me to ignore the searing pain I felt and go along with whatever physical indignity or agony I was subjected to.

A forceful shift of focus made a huge difference in how I withstood and ultimately facilitated my extraction to safety.

It's a lesson I reminded myself of time and time again during the long months of recovery. Feeling overwhelmed by the enormity of a challenge is a natural, human feeling. But it's also something we can override.

The impossible does not have to be impossible.

Once I was back home with Alicia and the girls, I spent considerably more time playing with our daughters than I had before the bombing. There is something quite lovely about watching children play and seeing how their focus rarely strays from the game at hand. Think about a child piling up building blocks, and how intently they're able to seal out the world and indulge their imagination. Not surprisingly, I had become more interested in mental approaches to challenges since I'd been injured, and I did a lot of research into theories about perseverance and singular focus, spurred on by watching my three beautiful daughters at play.

I came across a study by Karl Rosengren, a professor of brain and cognitive science and psychology at the University of Rochester. He once watched his toddler daughter try to squeeze herself into a doll-sized car that at best would have only fit her foot. Why, he wondered, was this child attempting a clearly impossible challenge?

The answer, he later determined, was that *she didn't know it was impossible.*

Rosengren concluded that children sometimes attempt physically impossible tasks because of something called *scale error.* As infants develop motor and cognitive skills, they can't tell the difference between a toy car built for toddlers and a similar-looking car built for dolls. The obvious scale of the object is not enough to dissuade them from trying to do what they successfully did with the larger car.

"This suggests children need to learn through trial and error and act on their environment to figure out what they can and cannot do," Rosengren concluded in his study.

I thought about how his conclusion related to me and my experience. I have long believed that the best way, and perhaps the only real way, to learn how to do anything is by doing it. Which also means that the only real way to know for certain if something is possible or impossible is by attempting to do it (within reason: I'm not saying you have to plummet down Niagara Falls to know for sure it's a bad idea). Rosengren's research seemed to confirm this way of thinking.

Before we become anchored by the wisdom of our experience and an awareness of our limitations, Rosengren determined, we can only learn what's possible or impossible *by attempting to do it.*

Then I imagined: What if adults could harness some of that early naivete and refrain from concluding something is impossible before we know for sure that it is?

Despite the enormous odds against me making it out of Ukraine, I couldn't possibly know for sure I'd never make it out. The default attitude we have as infants—that *anything* is possible—gets overridden by reason and logic and experience, but that only means it can be overridden again, through the force of our minds. I was able to overcome feelings of hopelessness and desperation, however justified they may have seemed, by making mental adjustments and consciously committing a scale error—believing that I was capable of anything until it was proven otherwise.

That is how I define adaptability—the ability to adapt our thought process to the demands of a new environment.

What I learned from my unlikely extraction to safety allowed me to quickly recover from the fear and frustration I felt when I was unable to answer the therapist's simple question. I knew from experience I could make a mental adjustment that would better prepare me to handle this challenge. I knew I could find a way through the maze.

I knew I could *adapt.*

The therapist helped me develop specific methods for overcoming my diminished power of recall. In the old days, I could hop out of bed and go anywhere and meet anyone and talk about any subject that happened to come up without ever once thinking about or planning my actions. It all just came naturally. But now it didn't, so I had to make a change. I had to begin planning and preparing for events in a different way.

I found that thinking about an interaction beforehand helps me get through it without feeling lost or helpless. If I have a planned phone call about something that requires details, I get as much information as I can about the subjects we'll be discussing, and I think about what I'll say and how I'll respond. Beginning the process of summoning and sorting through my thoughts ahead of time lessens the chances of me freezing in mid-thought or coming up empty. If there's a plan for someone to interview me—and I've done dozens of interviews since returning from Ukraine—I'll try to anticipate the planned questions, so I'll be better prepared to answer them.

I don't love having to do this. I much preferred it when I could do interviews on the fly and wing it in any situation I was in. But that's just not possible at the moment, so I've had to find another way to handle things, and I did—anticipating, making lists, plotting things out, being better prepared.

As a result, the way I schedule my life has changed. It's much more structured now. I need to know where I'm going, what things will be like when I get there, who I'll be talking to—really, as much information as I can get. If I know I have something big and demanding coming up, I will schedule a much lighter workload leading into it. None of this was ever a consideration before. Now it is.

The key to making these adjustments is being flexible and patient and, above all, positive. When thoughts and words don't come, I remind myself that some thoughts and words will take more time to summon than others. If something I try doesn't work, I remind myself that only by trying can I figure out what works and what doesn't. It's been a hard process, and often frustrating, but at every step I've learned something new that's been instrumental to my success going forward. I know I am capable of overriding pessimism and hopelessness and feelings of desperation by making strong and positive mental adjustments.

Since I've been back in London, more than one person has asked, out of well-meaning curiosity, if I consider myself disabled. To be honest, the question put me off a bit because I've never really thought of myself as disabled. I've been in situations where I've had to grapple with that question; for instance, anytime I'm forced to use a wheelchair (usually when I'm in too much pain). The first time I had to use one in London I was surprised by how few streets and crossings and stores are built to accommodate wheelchairs. Getting around in one in the city proved far trickier than I'd expected, and that was dispiriting. I was always one uncommonly steep ramp or elevated curb away from immobility, meaning I would need help to keep going.

I dealt with those feelings of frustration by thinking about a wheelchair as something I have the willpower to adapt to and improve at.

I accepted that it was just one of many adjustments I'd have to make—just one more facet of the necessary process of adapting. I still don't love having to get around in a wheelchair, but neither do I fight it as much, and I *am* getting better at it. On bad days I console myself by thinking about how much better an *electric* wheelchair will be than the manual one I sometimes use, especially one rigged to go sixty miles an hour and turn corners on a dime and zip me to my destination ahead of the mere mortals.

Adapting is all about finding better methods. If one path is blocked, try another. Purposefully commit scale error—don't let the size of the challenge get in the way of your certainty that you can conquer it. Making specific, well-defined mental adjustments worked for me when the odds against my survival were just this side of impossible.

Almost as impossible as squeezing into a tiny doll's car.

4

FIRST STEP

was three weeks into my stay at BAMC, in April 2022, when I first heard doctors talk to me about CFI.

That's where you're headed, they'd say with a smile. *CFI is an incredible place on the other side of campus. State-of-the-art, CFI. The best of the best. Wait till you get to CFI.*

Before I truly understood exactly what they did there, CFI—the Center for the Intrepid rehabilitation facility at BAMC—became a mythical destination in my mind, a place where miracles routinely happened. Later on, I learned the doctors were right about CFI, and might have even undersold it. But back then, just one month after the bombing and in the middle of several surgeries meant to stabilize my condition, I didn't have the luxury of dreaming about my next chapter—I had to stay focused on the challenge at hand.

Right around then, two medical professionals I didn't recognize marched into my room in the intensive care unit at BAMC. They introduced themselves as John Ferguson and Del Lipe, the head prosthetists at CFI for the past fifteen years. These were the guys who would, as my primary surgeon, Joe Alderete, put it, "grow back" my right leg. Back then, because of my TBI, my comprehension was still a little laggy and I didn't pick up all the details and plans they laid out for me, but there was plenty of time for me to catch up later. For now, John and Del got straight to work, removing the bandage on the stump of my right knee and wrapping it in some kind of cellophane that made a perfect cast of the stump. At the time, I did not realize the significance of their visit.

In time I did. You see, on the day they walked into my room, I had not been able to stand on my own in more than one month— not since the day I was found lying flat in the village of Horenka. I was quite literally immobile, confined more or less to my hospital bed, staring up at a ceiling rather than out at the world. I was like a newborn, delivered into a state of complete vulnerability and dependence on others just to survive. As long as I remained in that state, I wasn't, in my mind, really making progress.

I had to get myself back on my feet.

Of course, that was the problem—I *had* no workable feet. The right one was gone and most of the left one too. But the visit from John and Del marked the beginning of overcoming all that. That was why everyone spoke so highly of CFI—John and Del and everyone else at the rehab center *did* work miracles, in that they made people like me whole again, or as close to whole as I'd ever get.

I also later realized that the process of fitting me with prosthetics began even before John and Del showed up. By then, my kind and expert physiotherapist, Kelly Brown, had been wheeling me to a physio room, where I'd lie on my back on a low table and perform leg lifts to restrengthen the muscles I would need to stand again—quadriceps, abductors, gluteus maximus. In the one month I'd been unable to walk, my leg muscles had atrophied significantly, and building them back up was a slow and painful process. At the same time, Joe and Del were plotting out what my new prosthetic leg might look like.

The main issue was the small amount of tibia I had left after the amputation of my right leg below the knee. My remaining tibia—the larger and stronger of the two bones in your lower leg that connect to the ankle—protruded only five inches, or two inches less than was optimal for a prosthetic. Dr. Alderete had three options: elongate the existing tibia to create new bone; take some of the tibia from my left leg and use that to fortify my right tibia; or try to attach a prosthetic to the little bit of tibia I had left. John and Del, I later learned, pushed hard for option three. They saw my shortened tibia as a challenge, and they believed they were up to it.

On top of that, Dr. Alderete made the decision to accelerate the process of getting me mobile again. Patients "do better when they are ambulatory," he'd often say. He also saw I was gung ho to try anything and everything to speed things up. At the end of procedures and therapy sessions I would always ask, "Can we do this some more? What else can I do?" Wisely, my team of professionals pulled back on the reins to keep me safe, but Dr. Alderete figured I was mentally ready for the process of becoming ambulatory again.

Only in retrospect did I understand the importance of getting me up and standing as quickly as possible. Research has shown that amputees can experience a variety of lingering negative psychological reactions to their new reality: a deep sense of loss, damage to their self-image, PTSD, phantom pain, anxiety, and serious depression. Losing a limb is such a fundamentally altering experience it can scar someone for life.

But I didn't have the chance to dwell on the loss of my leg. The day John and Del came to see me, they made a cast of my right knee stump to use to fashion a crude prosthetic. A bout of septicemia—persistent bacteria in my bloodstream—cost me two weeks of physiotherapy time, but when I recovered, John and Del brought in what looked like a simple plastic cup, but which was actually a test socket that attached to my stump. After fitting it, they screwed in a titanium pole that itself was attached to a prosthetic foot with a gray New Balance sneaker on it. No one had prepared me for this, or even talked to me about it. But there it was—the first crude facsimile of what would be my new right leg.

"We're just gonna pop this on," John and Del essentially told me, "and then you're gonna stand up."

And that's exactly what happened. No time to get contemplative—just, *go on, get up*. Kelly brought over a sleek, padded, chest-high aluminum walker and set it against my hospital bed. Kelly also strapped a white belt with a loop on the back around my midsection; he would use that to help hoist me up and make sure I didn't fall. By then my tattered left foot had been fit into a big boot that allowed me to put a tiny bit of pressure on it, though most of the load-bearing would fall to my new prosthetic.

Then, in my tattered white hospital tank top and blue shorts, with my left eye still sewn shut and my left hand swollen and useless and my hair disheveled like a madman's, I sat up in the middle of the bed and with my one good hand grabbed a vertical handle on top of the walker.

And then, I stood.

*   *   *

I should say that not once, not even when I was on the ground in Ukraine after the bombing, did I think I would never walk again. I *always* believed I would walk again someday. I didn't know how, or if it was even possible. I just held firm to that belief. Nor did I fear how hard it might be, or how painful. Whatever lay ahead for me, I welcomed it.

That, of course, was just a mental exercise, a way to psyche myself up. But how would I feel when the day finally arrived? How brave would I be on that day?

Then it did arrive, and I stood up for the first time in exactly one month, and I know I felt a great deal of pain in that moment, but honestly, I can't remember the pain. All I remember is the elation. As much as I'd prepared for and anticipated that day, it was even more significant than it had been in my imagination. The simple act of standing was indeed the true first rung on my reconstructive ladder. The starting gun in the race of my life. It was when I realized I could make it *all* the way back, and rejoin society and play with my kids and walk my dog and laugh with my wife and do all the simple things I missed so much. Life would be different, that was for sure. I would never be the same. But I would recover. I'd make it back. I would be Ben Hall again.

After that, the challenge was progressing from rung to rung as quickly as I could. Just one day after standing, Kelly fitted me with my crude prosthetic and wheeled me to the physio room, where he held on to my belt while I got between two waist-high parallel bars and took my first step with my new right leg. It wasn't much of a step, a few inches at best, but it was forward movement. I felt unsure about what my left foot could do, and I kind of dragged it along as I held to the bars and tried to advance a few feet more. Yet I was so excited by what was happening that I took my hands off the bars and tried to walk on my own.

"Whoa, easy there, Ben," Kelly said. "Your stump is still healing. Take it slow."

One exhilarating step later, I said, "Can we go for a proper walk now? Come on, let's go for a walk."

Everyone laughed but I felt Kelly hold on to my belt a little bit tighter.

Then it was over. Three steps, maybe four. But for me, it might as well have been a mile. I walked. I *walked*. Was it painful? I'm sure it was, but once again I can't recall. All I remember is the rush of euphoria. A feeling like no other I've ever had.

Looking back now, I realize why that moment was so thrilling, beyond the obvious joy of making progress and passing a milestone. There was something else at work, something primal. We begin our lives immobile and vulnerable and dependent, as I was after the bombing, and then, at an early age, we learn to crawl, and take steps, and finally to walk and run. But we learn these things so early on we can't *remember* learning them. We can't recall the joy and freedom of taking our very first steps.

Yet there I was, learning to walk again, and I *could* feel all that joy. I *could* experience the elation of discovering mobility and freedom—of taking my first steps. What a blessing that was! What a gift I was given! To be conscious of the moment and its meaning, to get to immerse myself in it—that made me one of the luckiest people I know!

This became my mindset as I set out climbing the reconstructive ladder. Every step was beautiful, every rung a great reward. There was real joy to be found in the terrible pain and struggle, as there usually is during our darkest moments. One of the few things we can control in these times is our mindset—the way we think about what's happening to us. I know from experience that a positive mindset is crucial to recovery and rehabilitation, but I would go further than that—I'd say it's essential that we find the *enjoyment* of taking small steps and making progress, however painful and slow.

That is why, looking back on it two years later, I can now say that the moment I stood up beside my hospital bed, battered and bloodied and listing to the left but still standing, was one of the greatest, most meaningful moments of my life.

5

MAGIC STONES

Fall 1993

GILLING EAST

North Yorkshire, England

The start line was packed shoulder to shoulder with other runners, each taller and stronger than me.

I was the new kid, the slightly scrawny boy in black shorts, rugby shirt, and numbered bib, wondering why I was running this race at all. I was ten years old, and I had just arrived at the Ampleforth boarding school in North Yorkshire, on the grounds of an old Catholic Benedictine monastery. I had no business being in a race with all older boys, those from my own school but also from eight or nine other prep schools in the area. Yet that was where I found myself, poised at the start line, about to embark on a winding path through the moss bogs and thistles of the North Yorkshire moors, a deliberately rugged, off-track course with scruffy hills, dark woods, babbling streams, and old wooden fences, all meant to test our endurance and toughness. Or at least the endurance and toughness of the *older boys*.

The starting gun cracked, and I was off and running.

You see, my older brother, Barnaby, was one year ahead of me at Ampleforth, and when I arrived he had already established himself as one of the school's best athletes and most popular students. He was a captain of the rugby, swimming, and cross-country teams. Barnaby was only a year older than me, but he was bigger and more filled out, while I was a relatively small and thin for my age. Nevertheless, my brother's reputation became mine, and I was immediately thrown onto the cross-country running team alongside him and sent out on a multi-mile race with older and bigger students, in the middle of winter, even though I had zero cross-country experience.

Still—I believed I could compete. That was just the way I was— undaunted and undauntable. Sure enough, at the start of the race, I shot out in front of the pack, sprinting madly until I was way ahead of the next-fastest runner. I held this lead for what must have been a solid two minutes before the stampede began. One by one the older, swifter runners thundered past me as I slowed down to a jog, winded by my early burst. Eventually every runner in the race passed me, and I was dead last.

Around the two-mile mark, I hit a wall. My lack of experience had left me spent not even halfway through, and my eager sprint was now at best a trot. Then it started raining. After a while I saw another runner on the ground ahead of me. It looked like he was taking a breather but when I reached him, he went on and on about how he'd been stung by poison ivy and injured himself and how he couldn't go on. He made a bit of a show of it, trying, I think, to justify why he was quitting the race. I kept going and thought, *He's just going to quit? Just like that? Is that even something you can do?*

It never occurred to me that I wouldn't finish the race. It didn't matter that I wasn't a cross-country runner, or that I was younger and smaller than everyone else, or even that I was guaranteed to finish well behind the pack.

My only thought, even at age ten, was, *Benji, we will finish this race. Somehow, we will finish.*

So, I plodded on, over the moors, up the hills, exhausted but determined to get to the end. And finally I did, utterly drenched, muddied to the waist, out of breath, and seemingly miles behind everyone. There was no cheering crowd awaiting me, only one impatient race assistant anxious to button things up. It wasn't exactly a scene out of *Chariots of Fire*, but I felt great pride nonetheless.

This memory surfaced only recently, during the course of my recovery. I reflected on how I could have been so insistent on finishing a race for which I was underequipped, even though no one would have held it against me had I quit.

Where had that resolve come from?

The answer, I knew, was my parents. Roderick Hall, my brilliant father, was born in Manila to a Scottish father and Filipino mother, and was only eight when he began enduring the hellish, three-year occupation of the Philippines by Japan in World War II—a siege that killed one hundred thousand people, including his mother, grandmother, aunt, and uncle. Entrusted with the care of his younger siblings, my father survived battles and occupation by hiding in basements and other safe shelters until, finally, American soldiers showed up to liberate the country. In a final act of bravery and resilience, Dad gathered up his siblings and guided them through a hail of bullets to reach a squad of American GIs who eventually saved them. This became the founding plank of my immediate family's history—my father's uncommon bravery and resolve in the face of extraordinary danger.

When he was old enough, Dad enrolled and served at the end of the Korean War, and for the rest of his life he lived by a rigid code of ethics that boiled down to *what's right is right, what's wrong is wrong, and we must do what's right.*

My mother, Jenny, was the flip side of that. A free-spirited artist and patron of younger artists, she had a passion for traveling and meeting new people. She loved filling our home with fascinating guests and she taught me to approach any new situation with joy and gusto and expectation rather than apprehension. Together my parents gave me a strong moral compass (*quitting the race would be wrong*) and an adventurous streak (*you've never done this before, enjoy it!*) that forever shaped the way I approach new challenges.

So far, I've written about learning how to trust my natural resilience, accept the implications of an adverse situation, and adapt to a new environment. Trust, accept, adapt. To these I want to add a game-changing mental adjustment I've learned to make. I realized that accepting and adapting to challenges wasn't enough—I needed to *embrace* them as opportunities to discover new reserves of strength and resiliency, and to reveal my true character.

"Adversity has the effect of eliciting talents which in prosperous circumstances would have lain dormant," the Roman poet Horace realized all the way back in the first century BC. Eliciting new talents, uncovering new strengths—why *wouldn't* we embrace opportunities to discover these highest qualities of ours?

To again cite the American Psychological Association's *Dictionary of Psychology*, a challenge is defined as "an obstacle appraised *as an opportunity rather than a threat.*" What's more, the APA says, "a threat becomes a challenge when an individual judges that their coping resources are adequate not only to overcome the stress associated with the obstacle but also to improve the situation in a measurable way."

Think about that. We can transform an unwelcome threat into a positive challenge simply by trusting we have what it takes to overcome the obstacle. We can turn adversity into opportunity just by *thinking* about it differently. This is an extraordinary power to have—the ability to diminish the weight and gloom of a crisis, and strengthen our chances of overcoming it, through the sheer force of *thought*.

And I'm not just taking the APA's word for it. I've seen up close how profound the impact of positive thinking can be.

*   *   *

After the bombing in Ukraine, the hardest part of my journey of recovery was not my improbable escape to safety in Poland, nor the many months I spent pushing through my painful rehab at BAMC, nor being fitted for prosthetic limbs that I knew I'd forever be dependent on.

The hardest part of my recovery, it turned out, was when I re-entered the real world.

From the day of the missile attack to the day I came home to London—six long months—I essentially lived in a bubble. I was never alone; there were always people there to administer to me and feed me and support me. I had doctors and nurses and therapists checking in on me constantly, making sure I had everything I needed to get healthy again. I was wheeled here, chaperoned there, driven all over. I never needed to focus on a single thing other than my family and my wellness.

But then I entered a new phase of my recovery—the phase that would happen *outside* the bubble.

I was blessed, of course, to have the help of my brave and resourceful family in London, and Alicia and the girls all rose heroically to the challenge. But living again in the real world required a million adjustments. Everything was new—getting a glass of water, walking down stairs, having a shower. I had to find a new way of doing just about everything.

Even something as routine as saying hello to an old friend became a potentially fraught encounter. When I ran into someone I hadn't seen since before the bombing, I couldn't be sure how either of us would react. What do you say to someone who nearly died, endured polytrauma, and has a prosthetic leg? I began to notice a difference in the way people reacted to me. Some people preferred to ignore my injuries altogether and say something casual like, "Hey, Ben, what's going on?" Others would go the opposite route, comforting me and telling me how sorry they were for what happened. Some were overly dramatic, holding me by the shoulder and saying, "There are no words." Of all the reactions, this was the one I liked least. Were my injuries really so horrid and gruesome they defied characterization and weren't to be spoken of at all?

Most people simply asked how I was feeling, or how I was progressing, before moving on to some other topic, like, say, how my children were doing or the state of the Premier League. This, I noticed, was the most comfortable reaction for both of us: to neither ignore nor dwell on the elephant in the room—my new mechanized body—but rather to ask after me with a question or two, then move along to something else.

Either way, I was grateful for everyone's genuine sympathy and attention, and I took it upon myself to make these exchanges less awkward. I learned that if I brought up my injuries first, that loosened everyone up. "Legs feel better every day," I'd say, pointing to my prosthetic, or "Walking better every day in these!" Inevitably I'd see a look of relief wash over the face of the person I was speaking with.

They were happy I'd opened the door to the discussion because they simply didn't know how to do it.

Children, it turned out, were the easiest people for me to talk with, starting with my own daughters. Weeks before I returned home, Alicia began preparing them for what lay ahead, and they had a rudimentary understanding of what had happened—Iris, for instance, often told people that I'd been "bombshooted," while all the girls talked excitedly about my "robot leg." In the street or at school events, I had noticed children looking at me without fear or judgment, but simply out of curiosity. Many of them would even approach me and ask me what had happened. These were the easiest conversations I'd have about my ordeal, and usually involved a joke. "Yep, that's me, the journalist with the robot leg," I might say. "But you ought to see me kick a football now. Goes for *miles*."

To deal with this new and difficult phase of my recovery—having to relearn how to be part of the world—I made a conscious decision to not just accept every challenge I confronted, but to *embrace* them. To find the *joy* in them. That started with having to hoist myself up the stairs with my prosthetics off in our old house, which, as my daughters quickly showed me, did not have to the dreadful, shameful chore I thought it might be. When we moved into our new, more accessible home, we were happy to see that it came with a nice-sized trampoline in the back garden. One day I sat and watched the girls bounce merrily on their new plaything, and I had the thought that, before the bombing, I would certainly have clamored onto the trampoline and joined them. There was no way I'd have been able to stop myself from getting in on the fun. But now, I couldn't.

Or could I?

Early on after my return to London—and perhaps foolishly, who's to say?—I snuck onto the trampoline in our yard in my prosthetics and bounced right alongside the girls, promptly twisting my ankle and toppling over. I mean, I seriously bungled up the ankle. Couldn't walk well for days.

But even that didn't stop me. It simply meant I needed a new strategy. Now I take off my prosthetics and stay on my knees while we play a game where the girls have to dash from side to side without me—enacting the role of a troll under the bridge—grabbing their ankles and tripping them up. We have an absolute blast, *and* somehow I manage not to injure myself further. Accept, adapt, embrace.

In my first weeks back in London, I wasn't able to navigate very far on my own. In fact, it was probably close to one full year before I felt confident enough to leave the house and take a stroll by myself. Just walking down a set of stairs was difficult—I had no flexibility in my remade left ankle, so I had to land firmly on a step with both legs before descending to the next. Eventually I felt strong enough to go outside with the girls and walk a block or two (though it would be a while before Alicia allowed me to go much farther with them).

On one of my first days out with Alicia and the girls, we visited a pizza restaurant. We made it there just fine but as soon as we sat at our table, I noticed everyone in the restaurant turn to look at me. I was wearing shorts and my sleek prosthetic right leg was visible, and everyone—patrons, waiters, busboys—had a look. I remember thinking, *This is going to happen everywhere. There's nowhere I can go where they won't stare at me.* The old Ben could stroll into any shop and go about his business like any other person, unbothered, but those days, I realized, were gone now, replaced by a future of awkward gawking. And that was a jarring reminder of just how permanent my situation was. What happened to me was not something I could ever hope to undo. I was the fellow with the robot leg, and I was going to be that fellow forever.

That was the challenge presented to me as I sat at the table with my daughters. The question was, how would I respond? I have heard and spoken to a number of amputees who cannot stand being stared at; for them the attention is a hurtful reminder of the pain they feel.

Quite quickly, I realized I had to not only accept the extra attention but welcome it. *No, this is fine,* I thought. *This is what it's going to be. Go ahead and embrace it.* Trying to hide my prosthetic leg would have been like trying to hide a part of my identity, and I didn't want to do that. I wanted to go out in the world and let people see me as I am and figure things out from there.

At first it was hard. Being stared at wherever you go is a naturally uncomfortable feeling, not just for me but for my daughters as well. It meant *they* were being stared at too. "Daddy, everyone's watching you wherever you go," Iris said one day.

"That's okay," I told her. "I've got a cool robot leg and they all want one, so they're going to stare."

Embracing the challenge of my new reality, rather than feeling aggrieved or victimized, helped my recovery in a very real way. It took me a long time to feel comfortable with the staring, but eventually I progressed to the point where the scrutiny actually *bolstered* my self-confidence. By not hiding my prosthetic or treating it as shameful, I was able to avoid feeling somehow lesser-than and more quickly feel comfortable with the new me. My leg became just another facet of who I am, the same way someone's hair color or speaking voice is a facet of theirs. Today I wear my prosthetics proudly, and I hope I'm playing my small part in destigmatizing injuries like mine and fostering a broader acceptance of others like me.

It's possible that, on occasion, I have embraced the challenges of my new reality a bit too hard.

About a year after I returned home from BAMC, I was on holiday with my family in Sydney, Australia, Alicia's birthplace—only our second vacation together since the bombing. There we visited a pier overlooking the beautiful blue waters of the South Pacific. The drop down to the water was about ten feet, a fairly sizable jump.

The problem was, I *liked* jumping off things.

I remembered when I was a freelance correspondent covering the bloody civil war in Libya in 2011, alongside my photojournalist friend Rick Findler. Reporting the war was so intense and unnerving that Rick and I decided to head home a few days earlier than planned. We made it to a harbor in the coastal Libyan city of Misrata, where we expected to board a fishing boat, the *Jelyana*, for the five-hundred-mile journey to Benghazi, and then on home. But the seas were too rough, and Muammar Gaddafi's forces were shelling the harbor, so Rick and I took cover in a dark, abandoned shipping container near shore. We spent long hours praying that a bomb wouldn't hit the container, and we learned what sheer, cold terror feels like.

The seas stayed rough and the sporadic shelling continued, and to break the impossible tension Rick and I did something, well, stupid. We jumped out of our sheltering container, ran to the end of the port, stripped down to our boxer shorts, and dove into the water. The desperate refugees waiting at the port looked at us as if we'd lost our minds, which, perhaps, we had. But as long as we were trapped between life and death, between escaping with our lives or dying in that container, we figured we might as well do what we could to prove that we weren't dead yet. So we jumped into the water and splashed around like schoolkids and got out and dove back in and splashed around some more. At the time, it seemed like the only sane thing to do.

After doing backflips into the Mediterranean in between bombings, what was the possible harm in jumping off a ten-foot pier on a family holiday in my prosthetics?

Alicia, watching me as I contemplated the jump, said, "This is a bad idea."

She was right; it would have been safer if I just stayed put on the pier. Yet while I heard her say these words, they didn't quite register, mainly because I'd already made up my mind. My only response to Alicia was, "I have to do it."

Then I jumped and splashed into the water. I felt *ecstatic*. To be airborne and weightless and free for just a moment was utterly exhilarating, and bobbing around in the water I was beaming like a little boy. I felt so happy about taking the risk and doing something I love to do. I was proud of myself.

But on the way back up the metal ladder, I slipped and tore the delicate skin right off the front of my left leg. A large open wound, blood everywhere, bystanders staring in horror. I grasped my way onto the pier while someone found a first-aid kit and helped bandage me up. I felt bad because I never wanted Alicia and the girls to ever see me in too much distress. I'm not sure, however, if I can say I regretted diving in. I may have come up a little short of conquering the challenge, but, man, did I embrace it.

And it was *fun*.

* * *

In my time at Ampleforth school, I never made my mark as a cross-country runner, but by then I'd shown a bit of skill as a chorister. I started out in church choirs and then, when I was the soloist at Ampleforth, at age eleven, I was picked to sing the lead role in the popular Christmas-themed opera *Amahl and the Night Visitors*, by Gian Carlo Menotti. The production was in Nashville, Tennessee, and then in Spoleto, Italy. I moved to both places for four months to sing the role of Amahl. I hadn't thought much about that time in the many years since, but, like the memory of finishing last in that race through the moors, it resurfaced after what happened in Ukraine. Surviving a bombing and grappling with my mortality had a funny way of dredging up memories, forgotten moments of my childhood that now seemed strangely prophetic in hindsight.

At the start of the play, Amahl is a poor boy who limps around on a crutch, until his family is visited by three Kings on their way to see the infant Jesus. One of the Kings shows Amahl a bag of magic stones, and Amahl asks if any of the stones can cure a crippled boy. At the very end, Amahl is miraculously able to walk without his crutch, which he gives to the Kings to present to the infant Jesus as a sign of gratitude. As Amahl, I was basically onstage for the whole opera, in front of audiences numbering in the thousands. It sounds like a lot for an eleven-year-old to handle, but I was strangely poised and even excited to be the focus of attention onstage, foreshadowing my career as a network news anchor. I enjoyed walking out and having my voice be the one that broke the pin-drop silence in the venue. Unlike running in a five-mile race through mud, singing the lead in an opera in front of a big crowd was something I was good at and more than happy to do.

In one of the final scenes of the opera, young Amahl sheds his crutch, staggers for a bit, straightens up, and suddenly has the use of his bad leg.

"Mother, I can walk!" he sings in triumph as he prowls the stage, gloriously ambulatory (there's a tape of my performance on YouTube, which I politely ask that you *not* watch). Nearly three decades later, it was me who lost the use of his legs before learning to walk again. Strange how life circles around sometimes.

Beyond the obvious parallels, I discovered a deeper message as

I turned the memory over in my mind. Amahl was healed when a kindly King showed up with magic stones, which, as we know, aren't real. But the takeaway for me is that there *is* a certain magic that all of us can tap into to accomplish the impossible.

As I lay bleeding on the asphalt in Horenka, missing a leg and stranded miles from any help, the odds against me surviving—much less ever walking again—were surely astronomical. But here I am today, walking again, jumping off Australian cliffs, taking Bosco to the park, joining my girls on the trampoline.

My magic, it turns out, is my family. It is also my heroic medical staff. It is all my friends and colleagues.

And—it is my mind.

The power of positive thought is as amazing as any other force in the world. By purposefully altering the way I *think* about the challenges ahead—from something frightening to something to be embraced—I unlock a whole new level of ability and performance. This extraordinary shift doesn't just help me face hurdles; it also gives me the ability to shatter barriers that once felt unbreakable, and achieve dreams that once felt unattainable. No matter the challenge, no matter the odds against me, this simple mental adjustment makes a huge difference in how I confront obstacles. It improves my odds of *conquering* the challenge. It's lead me to discover new reserves of grit and resolve within my mind that are nothing less than life-changing.

None of us need magic stones, because the magic is already in us. By embracing the challenges we face in our lives, we tap into that intrinsic part of our humanity that is resolute and steadfast—the part that pushes us to *keep going, keep going, keep going*. And when that happens, as I can attest, nearly anything is possible.

6

THE FORKLIFT MOMENT

Alittle over a year after the bombing in Ukraine, I had the chance to travel overseas by myself—another huge milestone in my recovery. Fox News asked me to be a guest of the network at the 2023 White House Correspondents' Association Dinner, the time-honored annual roast of politicians that usually draws the brightest luminaries in Washington, DC, including, in 2023, U.S. President Joe Biden.

I quickly agreed to attend, and I was able to schedule a one-on-one interview with U.S. Secretary of State Antony Blinken for the day after the dinner. My health was good, my legs felt strong, and I could get around using only a walking stick, so it was all systems go. It wasn't much of a trip—a quick three-day skip to DC and back—but to me it would be an epic journey. I was finally getting back to what

I do best—traveling the world and interviewing people, getting the news.

Then, a snag. About a week before my flight to DC, I felt a sharp, persistent pain in my right stump. It came out of nowhere and I didn't know why it was happening, but I knew it wasn't good. When I walked, the pain radiated through my body and I could even feel it in my stomach. Even so, it wasn't the first time some random pain had kicked off out of the blue and slowed me down. I resolved to do what I always did when I felt intense pain—get through it somehow, and not let it stop me from doing what I wanted to do.

Which, in this case, regrettably, included a scheduled outing with my friend Rick Findler to try adaptive skiing in a facility outside London. Adaptive skiing involves hurtling down a slope on what's called a sit ski, which is basically a bucket seat attached to a wide ski. It would have been a risky sport for me had I been feeling my absolute best. But with a painfully tender stump, and my trip to DC just ahead, it was, to say the least, unwise. Rick, who came along to lend moral support, noticed I was struggling just to walk and gave me the chance to opt out.

"You sure you want to do this, man?" he said at the facility. "I mean, shouldn't you be, I don't know, resting?"

"No, definitely, definitely, I want to try it," I said.

There was a reason I didn't want to skip the ski session. My father taught me how to ski when I was young, and I wanted to be able to do the same with my daughters—or at least be able to get up on a mountain with them as they learned. For me it had been an important bonding ritual, and I didn't want to give up on it just because I'd been injured. Sit-skiing down a modest slope a few times was for me the first step toward being able to ski, in some form, with Alicia and my daughters.

So I was strapped into my ski, and an instructor got behind me and launched us both down the artificially powdered slope. After a few seconds he gave me a push and let me ski on my own. There wasn't much to the run: a few turns, a lot of gliding, and then it was over. It wasn't quite the thrill I thought it would be, which made me realize that what I loved most about skiing was being on an actual mountain, with real snow and a bracing wind and all that. Nevertheless, I did five or six runs down the sit-skiing slope, and afterward, I knew right away I'd messed up my leg.

Sure enough, I had developed a bursa—a golf ball–sized inflammation on my right stump that, as it grew, eventually prevented me from even getting my prosthetic on. The bursa became infected and caused radiating pain with every step I took. There was no quick cure or treatment; the prescription was basically draining the bursa and staying off my legs. I spent the next two days in a wheelchair, hoping the pain would go away and that I'd be fit to travel again. But the pain didn't go away. If anything, it intensified.

With just a day to go before my flight to the U.S., I had to accept that the only way I could still take the trip was to go in a wheelchair, something I was loathe to do. I didn't like using a wheelchair, and I particularly didn't like all the fuss that would be involved in navigating a busy airport and attending a crowded event in one. But there wasn't really a choice. It was either the wheelchair or stay home.

*　　*　　*

I want to share what happened next, not because I think I had an exceptionally hard time of it or because I'm grasping for sympathy or anything like that, but rather because I learned a valuable lesson that I believe is worth passing on about something that affects and impedes us all at some point.

Pain.

The first setback for me happened at London's Heathrow Airport, just before I was to board my flight to DC. A friend drove me to the airport but left me at the security checkpoint, and from then on, I was on my own. The tarmac shuttle bus to the plane was not wheelchair accessible, so a special accommodation had to be made for me. That accommodation was what I can only describe as a forklift. In front of all the other passengers who had yet to board the shuttle, a truck with a forklift platform drove up so I could be hoisted atop it in my wheelchair, then driven in the cold across the tarmac to the plane. The look on the passengers' faces confirmed it was quite the spectacle.

The bus beat my forklift to the plane, and by the time I arrived everyone was boarding. But enough people remained on the tarmac to watch the forklift raise me high in the air so I could be loaded into the plane through the food door, along with whatever other supplies were needed for the flight. Suspended in the cold, waiting for the food door to open, passengers gawking, I felt truly disabled for perhaps the first time in my life. I'm not sure which was worse: the insidious pain in my stump that simply wouldn't go away, or the humiliation of being shipped around the airport like cargo.

On the plane, there was no room for me to sit anywhere in my wheelchair, so it had to be folded up and put away. That meant that if I needed to go to the bathroom during the six-hour flight, I had to hobble up and down the aisle on crutches with only one leg. I did my best, but still banged around and nearly fell over more than once. Then I got stuck in the bloody bathroom. With only one good leg (with only half a foot at its end), I couldn't maneuver in the exceedingly small space and needed to be extricated. Once I was free, I was wheeled back to my seat in a tiny wheelchair kept in the cabin.

Still, I made it to the hotel in Washington just fine. But the room they assigned me was not an accessible one. That meant it hadn't been configured for someone with a disability and lacked vital accessories like grab bars, door assists, and adjustable beds. The bathtub was an ordinary tub that I would need to somehow wrangle myself into—again, without the aid of any grab bar. But there was nothing I could do except give it a go.

I stripped and crawled on the carpeted floor from my bed to the bathroom, pulling myself along, trying to keep the infected bursa off the ground and hoping to somehow engineer a bath. Dragging oneself along the ground is a challenging experience; it's not only physically difficult but it can also play tricks on your mind. It can make you feel lost and helpless and diminished. It is a harsh reminder of what you're no longer able to do.

But that was just the beginning of my "bath." I pulled myself up and over the rim of the tub, then slipped, ending up half-in, half-out. Cold water dripped out of the showerhead above and splashed on me, but I couldn't reach the shower controls. Unable to do much of anything, I curled up in the bath for a few minutes to regroup. Finally I gathered myself, used my towel as a bath mat, and somehow got out of the tub.

Wet and with no clothes on, strewn on the cold porcelain floor of the bathroom, my legs in continuous pain, I felt something else I hadn't yet felt in the aftermath of the bombing.

I felt defeated.

It was a strange, unwelcome feeling, and I tried to shake it, but I couldn't. The happenings of the day had left me mentally weakened. I had two important events coming up, but at that moment I didn't want to go to them. I didn't want to see or talk to anyone. I wanted to be home, not on the ice-cold floor of a hotel bathroom about to winch my banged-up self into the tub. I've always handled pressure well, but now I felt a nearly stifling anxiety that, coupled with the pain, made me want to find a dark hole and crawl inside it.

To paraphrase Marcel Proust, illness we pay heed to, knowledge we make promises to, but pain we obey. Pain is an uncompromising, merciless predator; pain *demands* our solitary focus and aims for our full surrender. The toughest minds can be crippled by the dense, hard, probing persistence of pain. As positive as I tried to stay, I couldn't escape this dark valley that my journey had plunged me into. To be sure, recovery from anything isn't linear, and there were times when my reserve of strength and determination seemingly ran out. No one is strong enough to sail through every challenge and setback. I certainly wasn't.

What I learned is that the only way to handle pain, absent a slew of pills that may or may not temporarily dull it, is to find some bloody way through it. The answer to pain is endurance. Since the bombing, I've felt excruciating pain on several occasions, worse than any I'd ever felt, and I've thought a lot about pain and how to cope with it. But I don't think I ever felt as broken by pain and loss as I did on the bathroom floor that night.

*   *   *

Later that night, I called Alicia and told her what happened. When we ended the call, Alicia promptly reached out to my agent, Olivia Metzger, who contacted Fox News. Together they arranged for me to be moved to an accessible hotel room the next day. The truth was that I didn't have to go through this ordeal alone—I had a community behind me ready to help in any way they could. Sometimes we forget how lucky and blessed we are to have loved ones we can reach out to in times of such distress. Thank God I had Alicia, who made sure I didn't have to endure another night like that one.

That morning, I tried to reset my mind, and I gave myself a simple pep talk ahead of my busy day: *Ben, just get through it. No heroics needed, just get through the day.* That evening I gamely put on black tie for the White House Correspondents' Association Dinner at the Hilton. I'd been looking forward to going for months. Many of my Fox News colleagues would be there, along with Sarah Verardo and two other members of the team who whisked me out of Ukraine—the naval surgeon and Bronze Star recipient Dr. Richard Jadick, who a year earlier dropped everything in his life to get me safely to Poland, and a highly skilled extraction specialist I knew as Bo. I was truly excited to see them all again and thank them for what they did for me.

Yet the closer I got to the start of the event, the more strangely removed from reality I felt. I knew it was because of what happened the night before. The anxiety, the sense of helplessness, were all still there, pulling me inward. From the outside I looked like the Ben everyone knew, the guy who'd recovered remarkably from his injuries. But I did not feel like that Ben. I was someone else, not chipper but sullen, not alert but disoriented.

Thankfully, I went to the dinner with Dr. Jadick and Bo, who made me feel entirely comfortable. Like the other professionals who got me out of Ukraine, Bo had a quiet authority and confidence about him. I didn't know very much about his background; it wasn't the kind of thing you could casually ask him about. But I knew without a doubt that Bo was meticulous in what he did. I trusted him completely. He was also as kind and friendly as someone in his position could be. I liked Bo and I was happy he was with me.

When we arrived at the Correspondents' Dinner, the conference hall was so densely packed it wasn't possible to wheel me around the dozens of crowded tables to get to my chair. The only option was to bring me around the back of the hotel and try to get me to my table that way. But because President Biden was in attendance, the security was highly elevated. Bo tried to wheel me down a corridor toward the dining area, but Secret Service agents from the president's detail blocked our way.

"I'm sorry, we can't let you through," they said.

I asked if there was a bathroom I could use, and the response was the same:

"Sorry, can't let you through."

Out of options once again, I had to wheel myself behind a curtain in a conference room and pee in a bottle. This didn't do much to improve the mood I was in. Then it became apparent that to get me to the dining area, Bo and Rich would have to carry me down a flight of stairs. They got right to it, hoisting my wheelchair and lifting me down the steps.

I finally made it to the Fox News table and sat among a stellar group of brilliant people—the Fox executives Suzanne Scott and Jay Wallace, who spared no effort or expense to help get me out of Ukraine, recover, and get back to work, as well as former attorney general Bill Barr and the outspoken NBA star Enes Kanter Freedom. The talk at the table was quick and lively, but it was obvious to me that I couldn't keep up. I felt the same frustration I felt at the lunch party at our friend Eugenie's home several months earlier, when I couldn't quite handle the quick banter at the lunch table. This time, at an event with considerably higher stakes, I racked my brain for something to say to those around me, but once again I came up empty. Finally, someone—I can't remember who—asked me a direct question, and all

I could do was nod and look away, unable to summon a response. My mind wasn't working, and I could not be the Ben everyone remembered.

Like the night before, I sat there and felt truly broken—and frightened.

My savior that night, once again, was Olivia. She could see I wasn't doing well and sprang into action. As soon as President Biden finished his speech, Olivia whispered, "Come on, we're getting out of here." She took charge of my wheelchair and weaved me through back corridors of the Hilton, slipped past security points, and charged out a back alley crowded with garbage cans. It felt like we were breaking out of prison.

Once again, I had been extracted from a tricky situation.

The next day, I had my choice of various events to attend—meetings, an embassy visit, a cocktail party. In the old days I would have tried to attend them all, but this time I stayed in my room and skipped all but one to which I had already committed to going. The event was hosted by Adrienne Arsht, a prominent businesswoman and philanthropist who funded the National Security Resilience Initiative through the Atlantic Council, a nongovernmental organization (NGO) promoting U.S. leadership and engagement in the world. When my Fox News colleague Jen Griffin originally asked me to attend, I was happy to accept. The subject of resilience was front and center for me as I continued with my rehabilitation, and even with how I was feeling, I still looked forward to finding out more about the initiative.

I went and met with Adrienne and others, and discussed resilience and tried to share my insights, all the while feeling less resilient than I'd ever felt in my life.

One after another, attendees told me how they thought I was one of the most remarkable people they'd ever met. How strong I must have been to endure my ordeal and bounce back the way I had. *Look what you've gone through*, they said, *and look at you now*. I was gracious and grateful to them, but inside I was howling with frustration. I felt like an imposter, a fraud. I was the *last* person they should have been talking to about resilience, because inside I felt so shattered.

I found it hard that night to even look anyone in the eye.

*   *   *

The next day, things got better. It was my scheduled return to the Department of State in Washington, DC, where I'd been Fox News' State Department correspondent right before I left to cover the war in Ukraine. It had been two years since I'd set foot in the Harry S Truman Building in Northwest Washington, and returning to State was one of my cherished goals during my long months at BAMC.

Maneuvering through the halls of State was far easier than it had been at the Hilton, though because of the injury to my left thumb I still couldn't steer my wheelchair straight. I tended to veer to the right and run into things. Somehow I made it back to my old office and met with many of my former colleagues, who very graciously applauded when I showed up. I understood the significance of my return—I represented the fighting spirit of everyone at the department. I can't say I felt elation at being back, as I'd expected; in fact, it felt rather strange. When I took the job at State, it was meant to keep me away from the front lines and set a new course for my family and me. But in the end, I barely got to do the job before the bombing changed everything. There was something a bit melancholic about being back at State, as if I were mourning something that never quite happened the way it should have. Had I felt mentally stronger that day, perhaps my reaction would have been different.

I was invited to attend the daily State Department briefing, which on that day was run by Vedant Patel, the principal deputy spokesperson. I wheeled myself into the press room and sat off to one side. Before the briefing began, a reporter from the Associated Press named Matthew Lee addressed the room from his front-row seat. Matthew was one of the veterans of the trade, a gruff, longtime foreign correspondent who wore a white sport coat like a character out of a Graham Greene novel. He asked that everyone acknowledge my presence, then rose to start a standing ovation for me. I was deeply moved by the gesture. The previous day, the steady stream of praise at Adrienne's event made me feel uncomfortable. But this was different. Perhaps because this came from my peers—from other reporters like me who had risked their lives in war zones—I found nothing but comfort and inspiration in their kind words.

I was also given the honor of asking the first question to kick off the briefing, something I hadn't prepared for. It was an opportunity for me to say something profound about war and journalism and resilience, but when I reached deep for a coherent thought, I came up with nothing. Instead I asked the routine question I'd prepared about protests in the Sudan. As soon as I asked it, I felt disappointed in myself. I'd missed a chance to share my gratitude and say something inspirational, all because I hadn't planned for the possibility of going first.

You should have been prepared, I scolded myself. *You should have been ready.*

Later that day, I had my one-on-one interview with Secretary of State Antony Blinken. I knew him from a handful of encounters when I worked at State, and we had a friendly rapport that I valued. Even so, I was happily surprised when, just a few days after the bombing in Ukraine, while I was under observation at Landstuhl Regional

Medical Center near the U.S. air base in Ramstein, Germany, I was told Secretary Blinken wanted to speak with me on the phone. In my groggy, pain-addled condition, the prospect of speaking with Blinken felt for me like a very small but hugely meaningful return to being a journalist, if only for a few minutes. That was a great, great comfort to me back when I was literally still in pieces from the bombing.

When I got on the phone with the secretary back then, I didn't settle for idle chatter. After he warmly told me how relieved he was to hear my voice and how sorry he felt for the loss of my colleagues Pierre Zakrzewski and Oleksandra Kuvshynova, I quickly began peppering him with questions.

"What do you think Putin's endgame is?"

"Will he be happy with the land bridge he's got to Crimea and the cities up north?"

"Why hasn't he hit Kyiv yet?"

I'm not sure if the secretary understood how important it was for me to be able to ask those questions at that time.

Now, a year later, I'd be sitting across from Blinken in the flesh, and peppering him with questions again.

"Ben, I can't tell you how happy I am to see you and have you back here at the State Department," Blinken said as we sat down for the recorded interview. "You are part of our family and it's just incredibly gratifying to see you not only back, [but to see you] do it with such strength and such courage." This time I felt honored and humbled. Secretary Blinken is measured and sincere, and he carries the weight of the world on his shoulders—when he says something, his words can make history. To have him so warmly welcome me to State gave me some of my strength back. But I knew what mattered most was our interview, and I thanked him for his sentiments and got to work.

I asked the secretary about the looming threat of China, his hopes for the apparently stalemated war in Ukraine, and the status of Evan Gershkovich, a *Wall Street Journal* reporter wrongfully detained by Russia in a small cell in the notorious Lefortovo Prison in Moscow (he has since been released in a prisoner exchange). The interview was short but lively, and when it was over I felt as good as I'd felt in my entire time in DC.

Still, something nagged at me. I was aware that the reason I got a rare meeting with Blinken was because of who I was—the reporter injured in Ukraine and now in a wheelchair. I wondered if I was okay with that—with receiving special treatment because I'd been blown up and was missing a leg.

Mind you, Secretary Blinken never once made me feel that way. After his lovely personal welcome, we slipped into the same kind of professional back-and-forth we were both used to at State. The interview was perfectly typical—me pushing for details and direct answers, him warding off intrusions he knew he couldn't address. I was proud to see the interview air on Fox News as a story that was less about me and more about U.S. foreign policy in a precariously changing world.

But wasn't it still true that the only reason I got face time with Blinken was because of what happened to me?

I wrestled with this for a while after leaving the State Department. I thought long and hard. The conclusion I came to was, in my mind, the only practical and reasonable one I could reach.

Even if I accepted that, yes, I received special treatment in booking the interview with Blinken, the real question was—so what? Reporters get interviews for all kinds of reasons—connections, doggedness, lucky breaks, chance encounters, even nepotism. There is no set rule for how to score a scoop. The bottom line is that it's incumbent on a journalist to take advantage of any and every opportunity that comes his or her way. When a door opens, you don't have the luxury of wondering whether you've earned the right to go through it—you have to barrel in and seize the moment.

Now, would I be happy if, in the future, I only ever booked interviews because of my condition? Certainly not. I would hate that. But who's to say that's going to happen? Perhaps I received special treatment this time, but there was no guarantee I would the next time. Journalism, and foreign policy, simply don't work that way. Generally, the news is not charitably doled out based on sympathies or obligations. The news will always be something that must be wrested out of the shadows by whoever can do it and by whatever means necessary. If you're in a position to get the news because of a loophole or courtesy, it doesn't matter. My job remained the same—prying information from its unyielding hiding spots. I knew how to do it, and I was still highly motivated to do it. And that's all that really mattered.

On my last night in DC, I had drinks with Bo and Rich at the hotel lobby bar. It was the best moment of my trip. Over beers, Bo and I gave Rich a little stick because he'd gone from embarking on courageous adventures like rescuing me in Ukraine to performing surgeries in a cushy private practice. "Hey, the pay is really good," Rich pushed back with a laugh. Sitting with these two amazing guys again, savoring the bonds we forged during my desperate extraction from Ukraine, helped me feel like myself again. There are very few people who can truly understand what our team went through in Ukraine or conceive of the courage and heroism that went into getting me home, and Rich and Bo are two of those people. We didn't talk much about our time in Ukraine because we didn't have to. It would always be an unspoken thing, an instant recognition of brotherhood and gratitude. I didn't need to pretend to feel any kind of way with Rich and Bo. The weight of what they did for me lives quietly inside us all, coloring who we are, connecting us forever.

*   *   *

Even with the reprieve of drinks with Rich and Bo, what I wanted most of all was to get home. I longed to be back in the safety of my home and the comfort of my family—my sanctuary. I couldn't *wait* to be with Alicia and the girls again. With them, my worries and doubts fell away, leaving me to live in the blissful moments of family life. My trip to DC had been difficult, but aside from not attending a few parties, I did everything I set out to do, and I was proud of myself for that. Even though I came close to hitting rock bottom and never truly felt like myself while I was there, I rallied and wound up with a solid, news-filled interview with Secretary Blinken, and that gave me a sense of accomplishment that was heartening.

My accomplishment was overcoming my pain.

I can offer all sorts of encouragement and inspirational insights into pain, but when pain hits, slogans and sayings feel hollow. It's like the boxer Mike Tyson said—everyone has a plan until they get punched in the mouth. Since the bombing, I've come to intimately understand how devastating pain came be, and how it can diminish you into a shell of yourself. That's exactly how I felt on the bathroom floor in Washington.

I also understand that pain is intensely personal: only we can know precisely how we feel. After returning home to London, I read a lot of studies and papers about pain theory, in an attempt to better understand what I'd gone through and how I'd handled it. I didn't personally undergo any kind of pain therapy, because I felt like I had a good handle on how pain affected me, and how I could cope with it in the future. Still, I wanted a better intellectual understanding of what pain was, and why I had survived it.

What I learned is that pain affects everyone differently depending on any number of factors. It's as if someone customizes our pain just for us. "As well as the neural interactions and links the brain goes through when a person is in pain, there are multiple layers of complex abstract thoughts and feelings a person has which culminates how much pain a person feels and how they deal with it," reads a report from pain psychologists at the Washington University Pain Center in St. Louis. In other words, pain is a different monster for us all, shaped by our thoughts and feelings and history—and how we fight off the monster will be specific to us too.

Even so, I learned there are established methods for coping with chronic pain. One is known as cognitive behavioral therapy, or CBT. The premise of CBT is that our reaction to pain is strongly influenced by how we perceive that pain. Psychologists who try CBT with patients study their thought patterns to determine if changing those patterns can lessen the chances of the patient suffering crippling depression and anxiety. "In studies of people with chronic pain," the Washington University report declared, "research has shown that CBT can result in improved mood, improved functional status, and decreased pain."

Imagine that. How we *think* about pain can influence how much pain we feel.

My research into pain therapy enlightened me on various other methods for coping with serious pain, including acceptance and commitment therapy, group therapy for chronic pain, and clinical hypnosis. And while I'm far from an expert on pain psychology, I can confidently say I *am* an expert on the pain I felt after the bombing in Ukraine, how it affected and changed me, and how, ultimately, I got through it.

I'm speaking now of physical pain, but not every challenge we face in our lives is of that kind. Pain has many forms, and it isn't always caused by physical injury. Self-doubt and helplessness can be painful too. Anxiety, extreme stress, and relationship issues can all, for lack of a better phrase, hurt like hell. Each of these issues has a wealth of scientific research into it, and is worthy of much discussion, but in the days and weeks after I lost my leg in Ukraine, and in the months after I made it back home, I focused primarily on the mysteries of physical pain. That's because I had received a crash course in pain and pain management that was more intense than anything I could have fathomed. I'd been injured before in my life, and I thought I knew what pain was, but I didn't. I didn't know at all. But I found out.

I found out during my ten-hour train ride out of Ukraine.

One of the many miracles of my extraction from Ukraine was how I made it the 428 miles from Kyiv to the Polish border during a shoot-to-kill curfew order in the middle of a brutal war *and* with a piece of shrapnel in my throat that threatened to dislodge and kill me with the slightest bump. Taking a car or plane was far too dangerous, and the commercial trains that were still running were already overflowing with Ukrainians fleeing the country.

Luckily, my extraction team learned about a top-secret Polish government train carrying the Polish, Slovenian, and Czech prime ministers in and out of Kyiv for a highly clandestine, high-stakes meeting with Ukrainian president Zelenskyy. Could they somehow get me, a foreign civilian, on board this railway equivalent of Air Force One? Could they infiltrate one of the most clandestine diplomatic missions in recent history—the first-ever visit to war-torn Ukraine by neighboring heads of state? It was foolish of my team to think so, but thank God they thought it anyway, and against impossible odds I *did* make it onto that train and safely into Poland.

It was a miracle, to be sure, but it was also the most painful ten hours of my life.

The doctors who treated me at a hospital in Kyiv gave me a shot of morphine several hours before they discharged me, but their supplies were so depleted from treating war casualties that they had no painkillers to give me for the long train trip.

Just about the time the prime minister's train left Kyiv, the morphine wore off and I became conscious of the pain for the first time since the bombing. It would not subside until I made it to Poland ten hours later. As I lay in the bottom bunk of a sleeper compartment, torn apart, stitched together, and without access to any painkillers save for a single Advil pill, I was vaguely aware that the only pain relief I was going to get was whatever relief my mind could conjure.

But first my mind had to struggle to even *comprehend* the pain—or, should I say, the different kinds of pain I felt. I hurt everywhere—the stump of my right leg, my ravaged left hand, the back of my skull, my face, my feet—and all this pain surged and rippled outward, converging into a volcanic, recurring, endless wave of body-wide agony. Then there was the pain I felt if I moved a part of my body that shouldn't be moved, or, God forbid, knocked against something. And there was the underlying, overarching, enveloping pain that never went away, that just kept throbbing like a heartbeat—the pain of having a thoroughly shattered body. The pain of nearly every system in my body convulsing with shock. This pain was distinct from my local pain. It rose from all points in my body in layers that flushed slowly to the surface before sinking heavily back down again, each layer somehow more painfully radiant than the one before. These waves of pain were so thorough and intense that each one promised to be the outer edge of what I could tolerate, beyond which I would surely cease to be conscious, or even alive. But these promises were cruel deceptions, for each wave, each layer, established a new outer edge of tolerance, and each new edge was not an edge at all, but rather just a random point on a seemingly endless expansion of what a human could handle.

More than anything, the pain made me realize there was only the pain and me and nothing else—no escape, no savior, no reprieve. Just more pain.

If there is a hell, surely I was in it.

As I mentioned, the pain that seemed utterly unendurable at the time was, in fact, endurable. I endured it for ten hours. It was a battle, to be sure, between me and my pain—minute-by-minute, hand-to-hand warfare with the most formidable opponent I'd ever faced. An opponent who refused to quit or slow down, only intensify, and who mocked the only feeble weapon I had to defeat it—my mind. In the end, I did the only thing I thought might help get me through the ordeal:

I *befriended* my enemy.

There came a point in the train trip when I accepted that the pain was not going to go away, nor was it going to be ignored. It just *was*, and I had to accept that, and go from there. Once I fully acknowledged the pain, I understood I was not in an outward battle against an external opponent. This war would be raged entirely in my body and in my mind.

So, I shut my eyes. I gritted my teeth. I consciously kept my mouth tightly closed so I wouldn't cry out or whimper. I walled off the world and cleared the battlefield. My brain still felt rattled and chaotic, the result of my TBI, and my thoughts were difficult to control, but I managed to find just enough clarity to make a key mental adjustment.

I decided that the pain was a *good* thing.

Here is the thought process I used:

Okay. This pain is real. It's not going away. It's not going to stop. It will probably get worse. I will only feel more pain.

But what is pain anyway? Why do I feel it so intently? Well, the pain is sounding an alarm. It's telling me something is very, very wrong with my body. It's pointing out where my body is broken and where it needs to be fixed.

The pain is the beginning of the healing process!

Okay, then. That means pain is a positive thing. Pain means I'm alive. It means I didn't die. And the more pain I feel, the more alive I must be. This is what it feels like to be a human being. Suffering is part of it. Agony is part of it. Pain is a huge part of it. These feelings mean I'm alive, and I should be thankful for them.

I should be grateful for my pain.

That's right, grateful. Grateful that my body is working the way it should, summoning the troops, rallying the forces, pumping blood to the wounded areas, firing signals to my brain. The fight is on, and pain isn't my enemy. The pain is on my side. My pain and I are in this together. I just have to let the pain do its thing. I have to let it be as bad as it's going to be. Doesn't mean I have to like it. God knows, I don't like it. But it's going to happen. There's no way around that. I can waste a lot of time looking for loopholes, looking for an escape hatch—looking for some way to not feel what I'm feeling. But I'm not going to find that. There is no way out. All I can do is get through it, until I emerge on the other side.

Ah yes, the other side. The place that lies beyond the pain. The place I have to fight like hell to get to. It feels like I'll never get there but of course I'll get there, because the other side is real. The other side exists. The pain is not going to kill me. It may try, but it won't. There will come a time, I don't know how long from now, when I'm on the other side of this pain, safe and sound. Which means the pain isn't forever.

THE PAIN WILL GO AWAY.

Okay, then. Don't turn the pain into something bigger than it is. Don't imbue it with indomitable powers. Welcome it, befriend it. Talk to it like an ally. Say, "Okay, buddy, that was a good one. You really knocked me out with that wave. Well done. But I'm still here. I'm not going anywhere. So do your thing. Bring it on.

"Come on, mate, is that the best you've got?"

*   *   *

I didn't know it at the time, but this kind of deliberate, focused self-talk—as simplistic as it may sound—is not unlike the thinking behind cognitive behavioral therapy. CBT hinges on changing your thought patterns—and for patients with chronic pain, research has proven that changing the way you think about pain can help alleviate physical and emotional stress.

So, did changing the way I perceived my pain actually decrease its intensity? Did I feel *less* pain?

That's hard for me to say given the groggy state I was in, and the difficulty of measuring pain. But there's no doubt that changing my thinking about pain helped me get through ten hours of the worst agony I'd ever felt. It diminished the *power* that pain had over me. My challenge was to navigate six hundred eternal minutes of insistent, granular, time-stopping bodily pain, and entering into a pact with my pain helped me rise to that challenge. It got me to the other side. It *worked.*

It sounds counterintuitive, but the way I tried to ignore the pain was by focusing intently on it. What I learned is that trying to escape pain, and being frightened of it, and begging for it to end, could make it even worse. It could add depression and anxiety to the mix. It could leave you feeling utterly defeated by the pain, and that feeling could linger for a long time, and continue to weaken and isolate you.

Instead, I thought about the pain and steeled myself to it. Later on, during a botched skin graft when an incorrect bandage was used and had to be stripped off, akin to tearing off my skin, I would await the next pull and think, *Okay, Ben, here it comes. It's going to be bad. But you can handle it.* Then the pain would come, and surprise me with its intensity, and sometimes I'd scream out in agony. The doctors would give me a moment, then get back to stripping off my skin. And I would think, *Right, let's get to it. I know what's coming, and I know it's going to be bad. So do the next one! Come on, I'm ready!*

In addition to knowing what the pain would feel like, I also knew I was going to get through it. I knew that for sure because I'd already gotten through it a bunch of times. *I can handle this. I have before and I will again. I can get to the other side.*

If you set up your pain as a challenge to persevere through, to *rise* to, and if you embrace that challenge and focus intently on it, rising to that challenge is a brilliant achievement to be proud of and to congratulate yourself for. It is testament to your toughness and character and resolve, and it has its own built-in reward—the relief of getting to the place *beyond* the pain. No one gives you a free pass to that place. You have to fight like hell to get there. You have to *earn* it. And that means you are fully alive because you went through this deeply human experience and you survived it, and now you are a different, stronger person.

A person who has proven to be *resilient*.

Like many, many people, I know that pain will always be a part of my life. With that in mind, I wrote a list of my hard-earned lessons— reminders that I am equipped not just to endure pain but to rise above it. Here they are:

- Don't try to ignore or escape the pain, confront it.

- Accept that pain can be an ally in the healing process.

- Convince yourself that pain is a positive, and force your thought pattern to adhere to that definition.

- Realize that enduring pain is a huge accomplishment.

- Build up an arsenal of endurance and inner knowledge based on all the times you got through pain in the past, and pain will no longer frighten or depress you in the future.

- If the choice is between feeling pain and not surviving, be thankful for the pain.

*   *   *

These days, more than two years on from that long train ride, I still cope with frequent bursts of pain. In fact, I feel some sort of pain pretty much every day, and for most of the day. Some days every step causes discomfort, especially days when I'm on my feet for a long time. I recently took a trip to New York and Kentucky and was on my feet for the better part of fourteen days, and by the second day I felt constant, stabbing, daggerlike pain in the fragile remains of my left foot. By then, however, I'd built up a fine arsenal of resolve and resilience, of experiencing and overcoming pain, and I knew I could get through the fourteen days—and do everything I was scheduled to do. I didn't have to compromise. I didn't have to be a lesser version of me. I knew what to do, how long I could do it for, and ultimately that I would make it through. In fact, I never mentioned the pain to anyone.

Please know that all these insights are not meant to disparage the use of painkillers. Of course painkillers serve a purpose. But I believe they should be used as a last resort. I had no choice but to get through the train ride out of Ukraine without any medication, but as soon as I was in a hospital setting, I was immediately put on some pretty heavy painkillers, and I welcomed them. I understand that sometimes they are essential to managing pain. But in my experience, the stronger pain meds made me feel foggy and out of sorts, less alert and less involved in what was happening around me. Perhaps that was the point, but I just didn't like how it felt. My training, and my nature, conditioned me to *always* be alert and involved, and drifting away to some murky state of being was, for me, only marginally better than being in pain. When I could, I weaned myself off the bigger pain-killers, until I was down to taking a medication that provides short-term relief of moderate to severe pain. Eventually I weaned myself off that too.

We all have the capacity to endure pain that feels unendurable. Not only endure it but diminish its hold on us—diminish the overall mental, emotional, and physical experience of pain. We have it within us to *resist* surrendering to pain, because we can define how we think about pain, which helps us find a way to endure it.

That is an *awesome* power to tap into.

Nor is changing our thought patterns an approach that only

works with pain. It can work on the many fears and feelings that tend to surface when we face large challenges in our lives—anxiety, depression, self-doubt, helplessness, despair. We do not have to surrender to any of these crippling conditions. We can fight them, and we can resist them. It won't be easy. It may take time. We might feel defeated and helpless sometimes, maybe often.

But it can be done. This is not some secret I've stumbled across. It's not some magic bullet, or magic stone, for that matter. It's just what I've discovered. We have the necessary resilience within us to fight through pain; that is our birthright as humans—as survival machines. We resist, we endure, we find a way through. It's just what we do.

7

FLASHBACKS

Fall 2023

Melides, Portugal

Alicia was behind the wheel of our black Land Rover Discovery, taking us to the beach on our summer holiday in Portugal. The girls were in the back seat chattering, barely able to contain their excitement, and up in the passenger seat I was in high spirits too. It was our first family trip since my return to London about a year earlier, and I'd been looking forward to it for months. Alicia steered us down a long, straight two-lane road that led to the beach, kicking up dust on a dry, hot day. I glanced in the rearview mirror and saw a white truck several hundred yards back, gaining speed. A few seconds later I looked again, and the truck was right behind us. It swerved into the other lane, sped up, and pulled alongside us to pass.

Suddenly—

Adrenaline surged through me. My senses sprang alert. I sat up in my seat and looked hard at the truck and I knew as well as I'd ever known anything who was hiding in the back of the truck and hanging off the sides, trying to catch us.

It was the Taliban.

Then, as abruptly as it seized me, the sensation went away. One second, maybe two. *Of course, that's not the Taliban*, I thought. *Calm down, everything's fine.* The white truck sped past us and went on its way, and neither Alicia nor the girls noticed my moment of alarm. It was a strange feeling, but also a familiar one—a flashing back to the state of vigilance and readiness I often found myself in as a journalist covering wars. This was the first time, though, that I'd ever felt that adrenaline surge in an ordinary situation. The Taliban often drove around Afghanistan in big white trucks, and often on dry, dusty roads resembling the beach-access road we were on, and perhaps that had been the trigger. But whatever brought it on, for a brief, surreal instant I was transported back to a war zone, under attack by the Taliban and needing to save my family.

And for that one instant, I simply could not be sure that it *wasn't* the Taliban.

I didn't mention the incident to Alicia at the time. Honestly, it didn't strike me as that big a deal. I didn't even see it as a negative thing. It hadn't scared me or driven me to take cover or anything, it was just a flashback that came and went. If anything, I vaguely enjoyed feeling that way again—alive, alert, in the middle of the action, like I had in war zones. I was never frightened or panicked in such moments; they were, after all, what I'd traveled all that way to witness. So I let the moment in the car pass and refocused on enjoying our family day at the beach.

A few days later, I was back in the car with Alicia when it happened again. It was another truck pulling up alongside us—that seemed to be a trigger, and for a split second I was on high alert and being chased by the enemy again.

It still didn't strike me as an alarming situation, but these fleeting moments of feeling chased and attacked kept happening, and eventually I understood that I had to tell Alicia about them. Not telling her about the flashbacks would have been hiding something significant from her, and I was never going to do that. Alicia had always been the one person I would turn to—no, *run* to—for advice and assurance and support. She was the center that held everything together, and keeping her out of the loop about anything having to do with my recovery made no sense. I just had to get past the idea that being open with her meant being a burden to her. I had to admit I could be vulnerable, and that it wasn't just me who was going through this experience, it was *all* of us—Alicia, the girls, and me.

One day, when it happened again, I casually turned to Alicia and said, "By the way, you know that big truck that just passed us? Well, just for a second I thought it was the Taliban. Isn't that something?"

Alicia was surprised. She had no idea I sometimes flashed back to my time in combat zones, and she asked me how often it occurred. I told her it had happened a few times, but I didn't think it was a big deal, which was true—I *didn't* think it was anything to worry about. Alicia agreed that reexperiencing sensations I had as a journalist sort of came with the territory: it was just part of my experience, my reality. But from the look of surprise and concern on her face, I knew it was a bit of a bigger deal than I'd been willing to admit.

We talked about it again later that day, in a quieter moment. We both understood this was something we had to watch and stay on top of, much like my lingering physical issues. But to me, I had already passed the biggest hurdle of all—telling Alicia about it. The important thing, the *crucial* thing, was that I chose *not* to confront it alone.

*   *   *

I was raised to take things in stride and silently endure. My father was that way; he rarely spoke about the horrible ordeals of his youth, a time when he was separated from his mother, grandparents, and other relatives by the occupying Japanese forces in the Philippines during World War II, and later learned they would all be killed.

Nor did he spin stories about his time as a U.S. soldier during the end of the Korean War. He adhered to a code of conduct that required quiet, dignified resolve. He did not tolerate complaining or excuse-making. That is why, when I was thrown into the moors for that grueling race at Ampleforth boarding school, I was so surprised to see a student not only quit the race but also carry on explaining why he was quitting. Because of my father, the idea of quitting and complaining was completely alien to me.

Some of that, I suppose, is typical English stoicism. Stiff upper lip. Keep calm and carry on. But as I grew up, I also came to believe that nothing at all could be gained by whining or making excuses. I saw it as a waste of time that interfered with forward progress. Certainly, in my work as a journalist, excuses were utterly pointless. You either got the story, or you didn't. There was no other box to tick.

After the bombing in Ukraine, my resolve to grit my teeth and just crack on only intensified. Two days after the missiles struck, during the ten hours I spent on the train to Poland with no medication and in excruciating pain, I made the conscious decision to not let any of my rescuers see just how miserable I was. *What good would advertising my pain do me?* I reasoned. *It would only make me more of a burden. It would only slow us down.* When Dr. Jadick, the naval surgeon traveling with us, asked me to rate my pain on a scale of 1 to 10, I answered 5, only because if I'd said 1 or 2, he'd have known I was lying. As it was, he knew I was lying anyway. His experience with combat injuries and the limits of human tolerance made him certain my pain level was at least a 9.

Yet even then, right after the bombing, I believed the key to my survival and recovery was staying strong and suffering quietly. I didn't say, *Okay Ben, you can do this all by yourself.* I wasn't so arrogant or misguided to think I wouldn't need many, many layers of support and professional intervention to build myself back up. I just wanted to avoid ever being a drain on anyone's energy and focus. I didn't want to waste their time going on and on about my pain. I believed that revealing the extent of my pain and anguish to anyone was akin to surrendering self-control, and I wasn't willing to do that.

At BAMC, a psychologist dropped by my room at least once a week to say hello and ask me a few questions and, in general, to "read" me—to see how I was coping with the mental aspects of my recovery. And each week I told him I was doing pretty well, which was true. He made it clear he was always available if I wanted to talk more about what happened, but I never took him up on that offer. At the CFI rehab center in Texas, I went so far as to occasionally hide my pain from my physical therapist, to make it more likely he'd approve of my early exit from the center. I would turn a corner and wait until I was out of his sight before collapsing into my wheelchair in agony.

When I returned to Alicia and the girls in London, I stuck to that approach of being as stoically unobtrusive as I could be. I did not want to disrupt the delicate framework Alicia had heroically created and maintained for our family in my six-month absence by suddenly turning all the focus on me and my needs. As limited as I was in terms of mobility, I was determined to go with the flow and, as best I could, pick up where I'd left off as the man of the house.

One evening, while Alicia and I were putting the girls to bed, the smoke detectors went off. Without hesitation, I grabbed our three-step ladder and, in my prosthetics, moved it into place so I could climb up and shut off the alarms.

"Don't do it," Alicia warned.

"Why not? I can do this."

"Just don't, Benji. Come on, you'll fall."

But I climbed up anyway and turned off the alarm and removed it and wobbled my way back down without crashing in a heap on the floor. Afterward, Alicia didn't say anything, but we looked at each other and smiled, acknowledging that the risk I took was unnecessary at best and absolutely bonkers at worst (imagine I'd wrecked my leg climbing a three-step ladder). Of course, Alicia well understood why I did it—because I *had* to.

For me, stoically enduring pain and setbacks worked. It made sense, and, I believed, it made all our lives easier. Taking on solitary challenges and relying solely on my wiles had always been who I was as a journalist, and I saw no reason to change that. Whatever came my way, I could handle it.

Today my thinking has changed. In the last two years I've learned a lot of things about what it takes to survive and overcome adversity and tragedy—chief among them the perils of keeping too stiff an upper lip.

*   *   *

In the months following my return from BAMC in late 2022, I started researching different aspects of my recovery, hoping for greater insight into the process of becoming, in essence, the new me. One of the areas that really intrigued me was the role of community in the rehabilitation process. I knew it played a significant part, because I'd seen what my remarkable community at BAMC—doctors, nurses, therapists, other patients—did for me. But I still wondered if personal resolve was more important to recovery than welcoming help from your community. I sought out people who had gone through situations similar to mine and I asked them for their opinions on the matter.

Some of the conversations happened organically. Some were set up through a project I successfully pitched to Fox News—a podcast called *Searching for Heroes*. The podcast allows me to interview others who have faced great adversity and glean from them new perspectives and ideas about the process I was undergoing.

For the podcast I interviewed a courageous woman named Kim Colegrove. Kim's husband, Jim Colegrove, was an officer of the law. The son, grandson, and nephew of police officers, Jim started out as a uniformed cop for the St. Louis Metropolitan Police Department before becoming a special agent and federal investigator with the U.S. Department of Agriculture Inspector General's Office. After thirty years of heroic service, Jim finally retired in 2014, at the age of fifty-one, to launch a new business and spend more time with his wife, four daughters, and three stepchildren.

Three months later, Jim took his own life.

When Kim and I spoke, we discussed the harm of dealing with trauma by stuffing it away inside. Her husband's suicide, she told me, was "shocking beyond belief. Outwardly, Jim seemed ready to retire. What I know now is that in the year leading up to his retirement, so much of the pain and stress and trauma that he'd held in, stuffed down, and compartmentalized for thirty years started to just rush to the surface. So much that he could no longer hold it in."

People like Jim Colegrove—firefighters, prison guards, soldiers, social workers, and others Kim refers to as "first responders"—often grow up and work in a culture that prizes stoicism. In Jim's case, a traumatic incident early in his career was left unprocessed for the rest of his life. In his first year on patrol, he was assigned to drive a squad car by himself, and on one patrol he came upon criminals who opened fire on him. As he had been trained to do, Jim got out of the car and returned fire, killing one of the shooters.

That event, and what happened next, left a permanent imprint on him. After the shooting, Jim was called back to the station, where a sergeant took his badge and gun, and sent him home to wait out an investigation. He was only twenty-one at the time and living on his own, and he faced the aftermath of the shooting on his own. "This pile of traumatic events—being shot at, fearing for your life, taking a human life, and then being stripped of your badge and gun—he has to sit there with them, isolated, for a long period of time," Kim told me.

After the investigation, Jim got a call telling him he was cleared. He was given back his badge and gun, and sent right out again, solo, in a patrol car. There was no aftercare, no debrief, no therapy offered— just, *It's over, get back to work*. Kim told me those kinds of incidents are sadly very common in professions like Jim's, in which the damage of squirreling away the trauma rather than dealing with it is just the way men are supposed to handle things.

"It was really kind of that John Wayne approach," Kim said. "As long as they were able to hold up that façade and that tough exterior, that was their survival mode. Even if they were completely falling apart on the inside." Tragically, Jim chose not to unburden himself at home by sharing some of his darker thoughts with Kim. Like many first responders, he didn't want to drag his workplace trauma into his home. It was easier and cleaner to push down the trauma and pretend everything was fine.

I understood that thinking. I never wanted to burden Alicia with details of the horrors I witnessed as a war correspondent, or even admit to her that these traumatic events had in any way changed me. What I wanted to do was come home and just put them to the side. The last thing I wished to do was drag them back into my world in London. I wanted to be in a world where none of those horrors existed at all. What I didn't yet realize was that by *not* allowing them into my life to be processed and dealt with, I might have been causing other problems that were potentially far more damaging to me and my family.

Devastated by her husband's passing, Kim responded by writing a remarkable book, *Mindfulness for Warriors: Empowering First Responders to Reduce Stress and Build Resilience*. To honor Jim Colegrove's heroism and memory, she also created the Pause First Academy, a support organization that offers in-person and online education, information, courses, and other resources for, as Kim puts it, "professionals who are exposed to trauma and the trauma of others."

Kim believes that resilience—which she defines as "the ability or capacity to prepare for and grow through and survive and deal with adversity"—can and should be taught and nurtured very early on for first responders, and, indeed, for anyone whose career exposes them to trauma. She focuses on the skills, tools, and practices people can learn and use preemptively to build resilience and better handle trauma when it comes—tools like meditation, mindfulness, exercise, self-analysis, and therapeutic group discussions.

Above all, Kim stresses that first responders and others need to move past the stigma of dealing openly with traumatic events. For many such people, "you're supposed to endure a horrible, terrifying, traumatic event and then just carry on," she says. "That's been the status quo for a very long time. 'Suck it up, buttercup,' they like to say. So the initial encouragement is that you can't just move on from trauma because you *don't* actually move on. It just builds up."

Sadly, the forces that drove Jim Colegrove to take his life are not rare. In 2020, 116 police officers died by suicide across the U.S., three more than were killed in the line of duty. In subsequent years the number of police suicides has only risen. The statistics for military veterans are even more grim. In 2021, an astonishing 6,392 veterans died by suicide, an increase of 114 from the year before. That is more than 17 veteran suicides every day, or roughly one every ninety minutes. These numbers are all but unthinkable.

*   *   *

During my six-month recovery at BAMC, I didn't think too much about any mental anguish I might have suffered in Ukraine. I just didn't have the time. I was far too intently focused on whatever the next step in my physical recovery was. I'd wake up and think, *Okay, what do I have to do today to improve? How do I keep moving forward? Let's go, let's go, let's GO!* I was impatient, determined, and vigilant. I was on permanent high alert.

This intense daily focus paid off when I left the care of my doctors in Texas after just six months and returned to my family in London. As I mentioned, getting back home, I thought, meant the hard part of my recovery was over. In fact, I learned, it was just *beginning*. Early on, doctors told me that rehabs like mine normally take two to three years—two in the hospital, generally, then another long year at home—before a kind of plateau of workable wellness is reached. Once I got home, I understood what they meant. Reaching that plateau was going to take far longer than the six months I spent at BAMC.

As a result, even after I returned to London, I never stopped being on high alert. In a way, the flashbacks like the one I experienced in the car in Portugal were an extreme version of how I felt every day. The need to keep running, to stay on alert, became a part of my daily return, dictating how I behaved, not allowing me to relax, keeping me restless. I was stuck in hypervigilant mode—*what's next, let's do it, let's keep moving*. Every day became about getting better, trying new things, pushing myself. If I wasn't fully "healed," that meant there was something that needed fixing, and it was up to me to try new things and find a way to fix them. And when they were fixed, it was immediately on to the next problem. I was hungry for challenges.

Even when I was out with Alicia and the girls, there was no such thing as an idle outing, at least not for me. It had to be more than that—an adventure, a treasure hunt, an exploration of new things. What's around that corner? What else can we discover today? I was constantly on the move, every hour, every day, with no end in sight.

The most difficult thing for me to do was sit down and relax. I've never been able to manage that. I'd try, especially on Sundays. I'd pull up a chair with the papers and try to have a leisurely read. Sitting still, however, was nearly impossible. I had to get up and find something to do, something to work on. Reading a book or watching a series on TV? No, not interested. I shied away from purely recreational activities and preferred putting my energy into challenges that would improve and strengthen me. I believed that being hypervigilant was what saved me in Ukraine and got me through my toughest days at BAMC, and I viewed it as a real asset, a strength. Whenever I had my back up against the wall, I felt I could always find a way through the crisis and just keep going. This ability had served me well, and I was proud of it, and I didn't see it as a negative.

But in a way, it was. The problem was that I couldn't switch it off.

There was no other mode for me to slip into. And that became a real annoyance. I couldn't stop my mind from constantly racing through checklists of things to do or formulating more constructive pursuits. Even on vacations, I found it hard to shut off my frantic thought process and let down my guard. This wasn't me choosing to be disciplined.

This was something out of my control.

There was another problem. My state of hypervigilance was not just a response to my continuing rehabilitation. There was a darker side to it. Much of the time, I felt like I needed to stay on high alert in case something bad happened. I needed to be prepared for whatever threat or harm came my way. This was the mindset I adopted as a journalist in combat zones, except now I wasn't in a combat zone, I was in London, with my family, relatively safe from any harm. But the mindset stayed in place. My alert level remained elevated at all times, so much so, I realized, that I could be triggered into believing I *was* in danger even when I wasn't, as happened in the car with my family in Portugal.

I wondered: Was I suffering from post-traumatic stress disorder?

At BAMC I was given a bit of psychological counseling in the form of a handful of talks with a therapist, but it just wasn't something I wished to pursue any further at the time. Only later, once I was back home with my family, did I begin researching PTSD, looking for clues about what I was going through. The Mayo Clinic defines PTSD as "a mental health condition that's triggered by a terrifying event—either experiencing it or witnessing it. Symptoms may include flashbacks, nightmares and severe anxiety, as well as uncontrollable thoughts about the event." People with PTSD, the clinic says, "may have temporary difficulty adjusting and coping."

As a journalist I had interviewed many warriors who'd gone

through combat and had PTSD, and I understood how dangerous and disruptive it could be. I found the idea that trauma could cause you to lose control of your thoughts at least as terrifying as, if not more terrifying than, the thought of losing a leg or a foot. At BAMC in Texas, where I was one of the only nonmilitary patients, the primary focus is on physical reconstruction and rehabilitation, but a tremendous amount of time and effort and compassion goes into helping warriors cope with PTSD.

Yet for a long time I didn't consider I might be suffering from it myself. In my mind, I wasn't a soldier, I hadn't fought in wars, and anyway I was good at separating the horrors of my job from the rest of my life. Wasn't that exactly what I'd been doing for nearly two decades as a war correspondent? Compartmentalizing any residual trauma in a way that prevented it from intruding in my life? I prided myself on being naturally resilient and always in control of my thoughts and emotions. I was the one who was *good* in crisis situations: levelheaded, unpanicked, focused. I was the one everyone could rely on.

But was this just a façade I put up to hide the real truth?

I sat down and thought hard about why I was able to so thoroughly sequester from my daily life any trauma I'd experienced. My entire identity had been built around being resilient and capable and the last person in any group who would ever need coddling of any kind. I couldn't *stand* the thought of being a burden to anyone, and I made sure I never was. This was the central plank of my character, both professionally and personally—I was the one who could be given any challenge and, on my own, fight my way through it.

Even after the bombing, when I became utterly dependent on the grace and compassion and expertise of others, I held to this notion of being the *least* dependent patient I could possibly be.

But to do that, I had to build a wall around myself. The wall didn't permit anyone to see how much pain I was in, or how hard the struggle was—and that was how I wanted it. It was the same kind of wall I'd built around my experiences in combat zones, which I generally didn't share with Alicia, preferring not to drag my trauma into our home lives .

It was the same kind of wall I put up at BAMC in Texas, when Alicia and I discussed her bringing the girls and staying with me at the hospital while I recovered in 2022. I knew right away I didn't want to uproot my family and have them move to the U.S. just so they could be with me while I rehabbed. I didn't want my daughters to see me in the condition I was in, and I didn't want to divert my focus away from the demands of my recovery, not even a little bit. Several people advised Alicia that my recovery would go better if she was with me in Texas, but Alicia knew me, and she understood what I needed. In the end, we agreed not to take the girls out of school and further disrupt their lives.

The wall stayed up.

*   *   *

Then, in Portugal, I finally shared a bit of my inner turmoil with Alicia. That might not seem like much, but for me, it was a breakthrough. I had opened a conversation that would now continue, which meant I was no longer waging whatever battle this was on my own.

After Portugal the flashbacks continued, and they still happen fairly regularly, triggered by loud noises like cars backfiring, and specifically by cars or trucks pulling up alongside me on the road. Even at home, when the doorbell rings, I imagine it's someone who's going to knock down the door and invade our house and do us harm. I'm always a bit relieved to see an Amazon driver standing there with a package in hand.

Later that year, Alicia and I attended a New Year's Eve party in her parents' house in Sydney, Australia. Their house had a view of the Sydney Harbour Bridge, over which the night's fireworks would be launched. At midnight we gathered around the balcony to watch the display, and suddenly the deafening percussive *tat-tat-tat* of fireworks throttled the air. In that instant, it happened—the sensation of being in a war zone. Only this time, the fireworks didn't stop. They just kept coming, wave after wave, seconds apart—the same pattern I heard so often in places under aerial bombardment. Each new round of fireworks was, to me, another shell or rocket. *Here comes one*, I thought, timing the outbursts, just as I had in combat zones. *Yep, there it is. Now here comes another*. Unlike what happened in Portugal, this was a drawn-out sensory shock, and after a minute or two I backed away from the balcony and went inside to wait out the fireworks. I'm sure I was the only spectator there who turned away so they *couldn't* see the big show.

It was simply too intense for me. Too much of an immersion in an alternate reality. I wasn't afraid or panicked; I remained calm and in control. But clearly something was happening that I didn't much like, and all I wanted was for it to be over.

It was around then that I recognized a correlation between these incidents and a longtime recurring dream I had about fleeing a prison camp during World War II, being chased around a lake by soldiers or terrorists. In the dream, my pursuers are also shooting at me, so I'm dodging bullets as well. Sometimes I'm on foot, sometimes on a motorbike. I race as fast as I can, round and round the lake, in between trees, over jumps, and the soldiers come close to catching me, but they never do.

But the lake is round, so they never stop chasing me either. I am forever fleeing.

I believed I knew what the dream was telling me—as long as I keep moving, as long as I remain *hypervigilant*, I'll survive. If I stop for even a second, I won't.

I had that dream constantly before I was injured in Ukraine, but just after the attack, I stopped having it—but started having the flashbacks. Was the dream no longer in my head but rather bleeding into my actual life? The flashbacks in Australia and Portugal felt entirely real to me, as if the terrorists in my dream had finally caught up to me in my waking life. But these "terrorists" were just as illusory as the ones in my dreams. It was all part of an internal coping process I hadn't even realized was underway.

So—what to do about it?

As I said, the crucial first step for me was sharing it all with Alicia. I found a balance between the extremes of being a total burden and being utterly stoic. The balance point on this arc will be different for everyone in a situation like mine, but it's imperative that we all find it. Because, I now realize, shouldering the burdens of trauma by yourself is *not* what it means to be resilient. Resilience is availing yourself of all the support and help that is offered to you. The first step—being open to accepting help and support—may be the hardest one of all. But after that, it gets easier.

Kim Colegrove's husband, Jim, *was* open to being helped and did reach out to a psychiatrist to talk about his darker thoughts. Sadly, therapy didn't work for Jim. Kim believes that first responders like Jim are a unique population and need programs tailored specifically to them, including training on how to deal with trauma that is offered to them at the *start* of their careers, alongside the training to do their jobs. Therapy programs that involve group discussions with other first responders, Kim says, can also be effective.

I am sure I paid a lot more attention to the physical aspects of my recovery than I did to the mental or emotional ones. The priority for me had to be putting my broken body back together. After telling Alicia about the flashbacks, we talked about the possibility of me seeing a therapist, and I even dug around for the name of a good psychiatrist.

But so far, I haven't spoken with any professional about my flashbacks. I am completely open to doing it one day, but right now I feel I have a very solid mindset when it comes to my recovery, and I worry about tampering with it. I feel strong and motivated and capable, and even the flashbacks don't slow me down. I worry that sitting with someone to talk about my issues could interfere with the positive mindset that has worked so well for me so far.

I also understand that many victims of trauma say things like this to explain why they aren't in therapy, and the last thing I would ever want to do is downplay therapy as a critical tool for those in physical and emotional recovery. I urge people to be more open about their troubles and seek out mental health professionals and have the discussion about entering therapy. The alternative to being receptive to the help and support of others is too tragic to even contemplate.

Opening up to Alicia doesn't mean I let her know every time I'm in pain or feel bad or anxious. I still don't see the point of complaining. But when it comes to important matters, Alicia and I will always tackle them together. For me, there were two keys to striking this balance between stoicism and accepting help.

The first is what I'd call defining my core.

I asked myself, *Who or what can I count on 100 percent when things go wrong? What is my untouchable foundation as a human being? The one concrete thing I absolutely know I can depend on?*

The answer was obvious: Alicia and my family. They are my core. If you take everything else away from me, I still have them, and together we can get through anything. With them, I share a simple yet precious happiness and optimism that sustains and empowers me more than I can describe. Yes, there are times when I face pressures and stressors that knock me down. There are times when I feel less confident about certain challenges. But beyond that I have an overreaching, ironclad confidence that no matter the setback or challenge, my family and I will find a way through it. My core is unshakable, and I know to lean on it when I need to.

The second key is recognizing the importance of community. Besides your core, it is your community that can see you through the worst of times.

After the bombing, I was entered into the ultimate community, a group of people who literally sustained and nourished me and indeed saved my life—the incredible doctors, nurses, and professionals at BAMC, possibly the best reconstructive hospital in the world. This community was there for me twenty-four hours a day, just the press of a button away, and without it, I know I wouldn't be here today.

But I couldn't stay at BAMC forever, and in London I was embraced by the community of my family—Alicia and Iris and Hero and Honor. And in time I realized that my community in London was bigger than just my family. It included the teachers who schooled our daughters, the neighbors who pitched in and helped, the shopkeepers who smiled and kindly asked me how I was doing, the strangers who saw my prosthetics and offered me their place in line.

My community was *everywhere*. Friends, professionals, relatives, colleagues, college buddies—anyone and everyone. In my neighborhood in London, not a day passed without someone coming up to me and wishing me well and cheering me on. I was the beneficiary of countless small acts of kindness: a smile, a hand, welcome advice, warm hugs. And the more open I was to the support of my community, the more I began to understand how community works. Not long ago, I had a chat with someone I ran into and didn't know well, and I found that because we were relative strangers, yet still part of the same community, it was easier for me to be candid about how I was doing and feeling. At the same time, and for the same reasons, this person felt he could share things with me that he hadn't shared before.

"Funny," he said, "but you're the first person I've ever told about that."

What a brilliant bit of alchemy that was—two people driven to help each other by the comfort and magic of community. Community both gives and receives. When something bad happens to anyone in a community, the community rallies and tackles the problem together. People bring food, run errands, babysit, offer advice, or sometimes just sit and listen when it's needed. This is an incalculably valuable resource for anyone facing a difficult challenge, and to not avail yourself of it is to squander one of the blessings of being human—the truism that we care about each other, and we want to help each other, and we are built to survive and thrive in communities, rather than be lone wolves.

This is another crucial lesson I've learned—that because of what happened to me, I have something to offer others who need help. I am part of a community that assists others in desperate situations, and that is hugely meaningful to me. It has helped me in my recovery. On top of my podcast, I also give inspirational speeches whenever I can. Once I was home in London, I was invited to speak in front of various groups, including military personnel. This past year I was asked to address a group of eight hundred American military nurses at Royal Air Force Lakenheath, a station in Suffolk, England. Many of the nurses were young and had yet to experience frontline conflict or its aftermath, and their questions to me were variations on a theme: How can we best help our patients? What is the best way to interact with them? How much does the family need to know? Simply by sharing my story, and emphasizing how invaluable the attention I received from caring, dedicated nurses every day was, I believe I helped them better understand the outsize role they play for patients like me.

"Whenever I really needed it, I always had a nurse there to tell me, 'I got you. I got your back,'" I said in my speech. "Every second I felt like you were right there by my side, fighting this battle with me."

We all face hard battles in our lives, and for a long time I preferred to fight these battles alone. But the truth is, I was never alone. None of us ever really are. There is always a community of giving, caring people there to pick us up and fight alongside us and have our backs. It's one of the profound blessings of being human—the understanding that we care about each other, and we can help each other.

The only thing we need to do is be open to it.

8

MASTERS OF OUR FATE

September 2023

MERKUR SPIEL-ARENA

Düsseldorf, Germany

The goal, always, was to get back to my family. That mattered more, and motivated me more, than anything else. But even in the earliest days of my monthslong rehab in Texas, I had a secondary goal:

To get back to my *job*.

One year after returning to Alicia and the girls in London, I was finally able to go back out on assignment.

I traveled to Germany for the 2023 Invictus Games, a ten-sport competition for wounded veterans of military service, a cause created and championed by Prince Harry. In a spacious arena, twenty thousand spectators listened to the prince address 550 extraordinary athletes from around the world. "These games are not solely about medals, personal bests, and finish lines," the prince said in his speech.

"They are about overcoming any and all perceptions that have held you back, especially those you've placed on yourselves. So, here, this week, right now, you break those ceilings, you plow down the highest walls, and then you make space for what's deserved.

"Pursue," Prince Harry exhorted, "the limitless in you."

The limitless in you.

Those words resonate deeply for me. I don't just understand them, I *feel* them. In fact, the idea of limitless potential has been guiding me ever since I survived the bombing. It is the reason I wrote this book.

And it is why the assignment to cover the Invictus Games was not just a fulfillment of my dream to get back to work but also a profoundly meaningful opportunity for me to be around other people like me—people who've had to piece themselves back together and find a new way to live. The assignment ticked all the boxes. It was perfect for me.

Even so, I felt ambivalent about going.

A nagging question insistently ate away at me: Was I only there because the people I was reporting on sustained life-changing injuries, as I had? Was the story I'd bring home nothing more than a story about a disabled person covering other disabled people? Was this the world I was a part of now?

Was I a journalist, or was I the journalist with the prosthetic leg and foot?

I didn't have an answer. But I was hopeful the next few days at the Games might help me find one.

*　　*　　*

It was Sarah Verardo, a tenacious advocate for military veterans and one of the key organizers of my dramatic escape from Ukraine, who asked me to attend the Games. Sarah's husband, Sergeant Michael Verardo, her high school sweetheart, was grievously injured in two improvised explosive device (IED) attacks in Afghanistan in 2010, losing his left leg and much of his left arm, as well as suffering a serious TBI. Their struggle to get through his painful, lengthy, ongoing rehabilitation—he's had to endure 140 surgeries—inspired Sarah to become an integral part of the Independence Fund, which provides practical support and aid to wounded veterans (she is now CEO). Sarah also cofounded Save Our Allies, a humanitarian group with a vast network of military veterans, intelligence operatives, nongovernmental organizations, and other specialists ready to deploy to deliver aid to war-torn areas, set up local makeshift hospitals, and in some cases, including mine, extract people stranded in dangerous combat situations in foreign lands.

Sarah is an uncommonly giving, compassionate human being, and it is no exaggeration to say I owe her my life. When she asked me to travel to Düsseldorf for the Games to represent the Independence Fund and present medals to some of the finalists, I quickly said yes. I knew that Alicia and I were extremely lucky; we had the support of Fox News and access to top-notch medical care, something many of America's wounded warriors do not have. I speak with and visit my physiotherapist regularly, but I have encountered some amputees with prosthetics who haven't seen their physios for months. Many don't have a proper wheelchair or know whom to contact about supports or grants. If there is any way I can help others like me gain access to the kind of support I have, I am fully committed to doing it.

What's more, two of the competitors at Invictus were wounded vets who rehabbed alongside me at BAMC in Texas. Back then we shared our hopes and dreams for our unknowable futures, and now here we were, the three of us, about to achieve a goal we'd set for

ourselves in the bleakest of times. I was delighted I'd get to see them
again and catch up and compare notes. I pitched the story to Fox
News and they agreed I could put together a package on the Games,
which also meant more publicity for the Independence Fund. It was
a win for everyone, and for me it was my first foreign trip to report a
story since the bombing, as well as the first trip I'd be taking without
anyone like Bo to help me.

Alicia, as always, was my most strenuous champion. She knew
how important it was for me to get back to reporting, and she was
happy to see me take the assignment. She recognized what a perfect opportunity going to the Games was. It wasn't a war zone, it
was only a ninety-minute flight, and I'd be surrounded by others for
whom navigating new locations and situations was a challenge. If
anything, she worried about my stamina, and about how I'd respond
to having a full schedule of interviews in different locations on the
sprawling campus of the Games. To be honest, I worried about that
too. Logistics were always difficult in the best of reporting situations, and as a freelancer I was often dashing from here to there to
get interviews. But my dashing days were over. Yet neither Alicia
nor I worried that I wouldn't be able to find a way to successfully get
through the Games.

The thing with road trips, though, is that you have to expect the
unexpected, because inevitably something will go wrong.

When I arrived at my hotel room in Düsseldorf, I discovered,
just as I had in Washington, DC, that the room wasn't accessible.
As I learned from my trip to DC, the amenities in an accessible hotel
room—grab bars, door assist, adjustable beds—make a dramatic
difference. In Düsseldorf, understandably, the demand for accessible
rooms was so great that the hotel had given my room away to someone else who needed it. I wrote it off as a minor setback, but in fact

the experience was more challenging than I expected. Not necessarily physically—though that was difficult too—but mentally.

The big problem, as it often was, was getting from the bed to the bathroom without my prosthetics on. In accessible rooms there are ways to scoot yourself to the bathroom, but in my hotel room I had no choice but to get down on the floor and crawl. Early on in my return to London, I had done a fair share of crawling as I adjusted to my new reality, and I got used to it. But over the months in my new home in London, I hadn't had to crawl as often, and I forgot how difficult it could be—once again, not just physically, but mentally.

Now I had to do it for the next five days. My first night in the hotel, I felt a little twinge of how I'd felt when I went to Washington, DC— defeated before I'd even begun.

Yet it was my time in DC that saved me in Düsseldorf.

I've learned that the things that are particularly hard and bad and negative in a recovery process are generally only *truly* terrible the first time around. Once you know what to expect, you have an idea of what it will be like and how to deal with it, and from there it will only get easier. Not easy—but easier.

The key is making a mental adjustment—forcing a thought. And the thought is: *I will not define this pain or discomfort as something horrendous and unbearable but rather as the next crucial step I need to take toward getting better.* Once it's reduced to a single step, it can be navigated. You know you can get through it because you already have gotten through it the first time. You experienced it, and you figured it out.

Dragging myself across the floor that night, I had a choice— surrender to the negative, dispiriting implications that could have overwhelmed me, or turn the situation around into something manageable. Instead of surrendering or wallowing, I managed my perspective. I forced this thought: *I've crawled before and I may have to crawl again, so I just have to accept this could be an occasional necessity. Crawl on the floor for a glass of water? Fine. So be it. I can handle that. Just get on with it.*

And from that moment on, crawling along the floor never really bothered me again.

*   *   *

The Games officially began with a parade of nations: nearly 600 competitors from 21 countries vying for 666 medals in 10 different sports. One by one the teams emerged on the vast main stage, usually led by combatants in wheelchairs. They all wore uniforms with the bright colors of their country and usually an emblazoned flag as well. It was remarkable to see so many disabled athletes in one place: dozens of men and women with prosthetic legs and arms, others in wheelchairs, some still limping. And the positive energy coming from the athletes was palpable. If you watch footage from the ceremony, you can see they are bursting with pride and emotion and anticipation. Perhaps a better word to describe the looks on their faces is *joy*. It was instantly clear that this was their moment, something they had planned for and fought for and dreamed of for a long time.

They were, like me, making a dream come true.

I spent most of my time with the United States team—59 competitors, 29 of them women. As I sat with family members and team volunteers and coaches and medics—and as was confirmed throughout the Games—I was struck by how genuinely enthusiastic and spirited everyone was. I'd been to regular sporting events and this one was no different. There was an atmosphere of fierce competitiveness and determination and national pride, just like you might see at a

World Cup match. Hundreds of spectators were wearing their national colors or waving their nation's flag. I realized these athletes and teams were not just there to participate. Just showing up was *not* their dream. Their dream was to *win*.

In fact, they wanted to win the *hell* out of their events. Competing at all was a victory of sorts, given what they'd been through. But it was not *the* goal. They did not want moral victories. They wanted medals. They wanted to *exceed* any expectations of them. There was nothing ceremonial or performative about the events. They were as competitive and hard-fought as any athletic event I'd ever watched.

My job was to take in as many competitions as I could and speak with as many athletes as I could, mainly from the U.S. team but also from other countries. I had a few scheduled interviews, but I'd also be roaming the grounds, looking for stories. The events were archery, athletics, indoor rowing, powerlifting, cycling, sitting volleyball, swimming, table tennis, and wheelchair rugby and basketball.

Early on I watched Sergeant First Class Lauren Montoya of the U.S. Special Operations Command compete at indoor rowing. A co-captain of the American squad, Lauren was all of five foot three, but she had a commanding presence. A native of Austin, Texas, she was deployed in southern Afghanistan in 2012 with the 7th SFG operational detachment alpha team. She was on a reconnaissance mission when the gunner she was riding in rolled over a command-detonated IED. Lauren was pinned beneath the truck and its heavy equipment, and she suffered a crushed heel bone, a ruptured Achilles tendon, significant muscle and nerve damage to her foot and lower left leg, and a TBI. A doctor told her she would never walk well again, and after a year of strenuous rehab her left leg was amputated at the knee.

From that point on, Lauren never looked back. She spent two intense years rebuilding herself, regaining her strength and balance, fortifying her already impressive mental resolve. Fitted with a blade-style prosthetic, she looked poised and powerful. When I interviewed her at the rowing event, one of four events she'd signed up for, she told me she was "steadfast, resilient, and relentless." She was also, I could clearly see, buoyant. "Being part of a team again, feeling useful, being active, all of those things help with your mental health," she said. "You're getting back to the gym. You're getting back to *work*."

U.S. Marine Corps Corporal Kionte Storey lost his right leg when he stepped on an IED in Afghanistan in 2010. I spoke with him as he prepared to compete in a track meet. "I found myself in a really dark place," he told me about his injury. "I was abusing my pain medication, and I didn't want to deal with life. I had to find my way out of the darkness, and sports was my way out." I heard this sentiment many times that week—the idea that preparing for competition literally saved lives. I understood this, because I know how important it is to be able to steer *all* your focus onto one consuming task. Whether it's sports or community outreach or simply getting home to see your family, the ability to be singularly focused on one goal is almost like a superpower—it imbues us with strength and resolve beyond what we ordinarily might be able to access.

U.S. Air Force Technical Sergeant Kevin Greene was competing in five different sports, and I watched him play wheelchair basketball. After the game I caught up with him and asked him what the Invictus Games meant to him. "These games give you *life*," he said. "But they also help you curate a lifestyle for yourself to help you live your life post-injury." Best of all, he went on, "they give you a chance to don the uniform again."

That was another sentiment I heard often at the Games—how happy these wounded veterans were to represent the U.S. and wear a U.S. uniform again. There was no bitterness, no resentment, no dwelling on the past, just pride and determination and above all the enormous satisfaction of being part of a team again. Retired Technical Sergeant Chris Ferrell, who was deployed to Iraq and Afghanistan six times and suffered severe PTSD after an IED explosion, discussed the significance of the team aspect of the Games when we spoke. "When you start hitting those low points, those dark spaces in your life, and then you're blessed enough to come here and be around all these other warriors, it just reaffirms why you're here and why you need to continue to spread the message," he explained. The message he was spreading?

This is not something you have to battle alone.

There was one athlete I was especially keen to reconnect with—U.S. Air Force Master Sergeant Justin James, whom I first met when we rehabbed at BAMC, and specifically when we were treated at the hospital's world-renowned prosthetics program, CFI.

Justin joined the U.S. Air Force as a maintenance journeyman patching up military vehicles, and eventually became a combat controller, providing tactical support on more than four hundred missions. He was injured in Afghanistan when he crushed his left foot in a parachuting accident. At BAMC, my chief surgeon, Dr. Alderete, asked Justin to visit me in my room and talk about what was likely in store for me. In a way, Justin was my welcoming committee, gently ushering me into the world of missing limbs and prosthetics. Our talks were one of the highlights of my time at IFC, with Justin selflessly sharing his powerful insights and wisdom. We became good friends.

To compete at the Invictus Games, he wore a curved, carbon-fiber, blade-style prosthetic. Stocky and athletic, with a slightly graying beard and kind eyes, Justin was a model of integrity and selfless dignity. "There's always someone who has got it worse," he said before the Games. "I'm still the same person I was before my injury." He spoke often about the value of resilience, both in the military and the rehabilitation process. "It plays a huge role in your recovery," he said. "If you have resolve, you can tackle anything."

Justin and I talked on the phone before the Games, comparing our levels of excitement about fulfilling the dreams we shared with each other at BAMC. We finally met up at the volleyball courts at one end of Merkur Spiel-Arena, and we gave each other a big hug. Then I sat in the stands with members of his family and the U.S. contingent and watched him compete in the volleyball event.

Up in the stands someone handed me a small American flag, and I took it and waved it and cheered throughout the entire match. I was lost in the moment, and in footage of me from the event I look like a little boy cheering on his favorite team. It was simply one of the most exhilarating moments of my life.

Why? Because of how *normal* it was.

This was a sacred ritual of life as we know it—watching others compete, cheering them on, reveling in their victories, being *part* of it all. From the ancient Greeks honoring Zeus by gathering in the Peloponnese to root on runners, wrestlers, and discus throwers competing for olive wreaths, to Texas families tailgating and packing bleachers to fire up gung ho high schoolers in their time-honored Friday night football games, humans have long cherished the sheer elation of witnessing competition. There is something elemental about it, and important—it is how we demonstrate our highest values and deepest strengths. The Invictus Games were no different, and perhaps even more poignant and profound. We weren't just cheering on Justin James and the other courageous wounded veterans—we were celebrating the unconquerability of the human mind and spirit.

This is great, I thought as I sat in the stands. *This is awesome. All of us together, cheering on these athletes, being part of a defining moment, being part of a community. This is what it's all about. I love this.*

I was homing in on the very heart of the Games, the reason I was there—the higher purpose that, ever since getting back home from BAMC, had so far eluded me.

*   *   *

The hardest part of covering the Games, as both Alicia and I had suspected, was keeping up with the schedule. My days were constant jumbles of interviews, live hits, events, and appearances. You are here, talking to someone, then *boom*—you're across the sprawling campus of the Games, talking to someone else. Before the bombing, this was the part of the job I loved: its breathless, adrenalized pace. But now things were different. I simply couldn't get from point A to point B as easily or as quickly as I once had. The satisfaction of completing an assignment was still there, and I was zipping around the campus as quickly as I could on my prosthetic leg, but I had to accept that I might only get to do four or five interviews, and not the seven or eight I would have done in the old days.

On only my second day there, I began to feel intense pain in my legs, particularly in my partially reconstructed left foot. A shooting, burning, radiating pain. I wasn't used to this much walking and standing. Knowing I had to keep to my schedule, and bounce from event to event, forced me to confront the pain in a way that wouldn't mean stopping and sitting down and resting, which I didn't have time for. I either had to keep up the frantic pace or quit altogether.

And I wasn't going to quit.

Instead, I made a mental adjustment—another forced thought.

The thought was this: *screw the pain.*

I made a very conscious decision on my second day in Düsseldorf that I was not going to let the pain interfere with anything I'd been sent there to do. I would interview everyone and attend every event and tell every story I'd planned to. I would push *through* the pain. Again, this may sound simplistic, but it's exactly what I did. As scheduled, I was at the medal ceremony after the archery competition to present medals to the finalists—including U.S. Air Force Technical Sergeant Jessica Garcia, a highly skilled archer who won a silver medal. When I went back to watch footage of the ceremony, I could tell from my expression that I was tired and likely in a lot of pain. I don't think anyone else could tell, but I could. In any case, I was present and engaged and genuinely excited to celebrate these crowning moments with Jessica and the other athletes. I knew it wasn't going to be easy, and it wasn't. It was hard work. Trying to ignore pain is a challenge unlike any other.

But I was lucky—I was in a position to draw much-needed inspiration from all the relentless fighters around me, like Sergeant Garcia.

On my way out of the Games, I saw one American athlete with a prosthetic leg standing off by himself near one of the exits. He seemed confused. I learned he'd suffered a severe TBI and, like me, sometimes had trouble remembering things. He knew he was supposed to be somewhere and meet someone and do something, he just couldn't summon the specifics. So he just stood there, looking lost. I knew how he must have felt and I went over to him, because I didn't want him to feel all alone.

What struck me most as I waited with him was how patient he remained. It would have been easy for him to feel abandoned and alone, cut off from his support staff, cut off from everyone. But he gave the impression this was not the first time he'd been stranded and unable to figure out what he was supposed to do. In that situation again, thousands of miles from home in a foreign country, he kept his cool. He checked his phone. He didn't get flustered. He turned to me and said, "Hey, sometimes this gets the better of me, you know? I just have to wait and figure it out. It's just how it is."

Before long, someone did show up to meet him and take him to his next destination. I found the few minutes I spent with him extremely inspiring. He was having his problems, same as I was having mine. But he was patient and he figured it out. That's what we humans are really good at—*figuring things out*. There is always a path through the worst of our predicaments, no matter how desperate we may feel, and given time we will figure out what that path is. We always do.

On the last day of competition, I told my Fox News producer and cameraman I needed to tend to an errand. In fact, there was something I needed to figure out, and I needed time alone to do it. The Games were nearing an end and I remembered the nagging questions I'd been wrestling with since I arrived in Düsseldorf. It was time to push the issue and find some answers.

I sat off by myself in the stands at Merkur Spiel-Arena and watched a wheelchair rugby match. I focused on the combatants, and how passionate they were. I focused on the physicality of what they were doing, and on their powerful competitive drive. I tried to tap into what, precisely, they were so fiercely determined to achieve. At that moment, I didn't want to be a reporter. I didn't want to be the wounded guy writing about other wounded people. I just wanted to sit and watch and figure out what it all meant to me.

I thought about how all the athletes who made it to the Games, and thousands more who didn't, had a story. What I was watching was just a snapshot of a much broader narrative. Every one of them had gone through years of struggle and setbacks and hardship. Isolated minutes and hours and days of extreme challenges. Some had felt so damaged and broken that they gave up. Some tried to take their own lives. Their stories were long and specific and personal and not always positive.

Yet here they were, very much alive, very much engaged, reaching deep to summon new reserves of strength. They were fighters, and now they were fighting again, this time to reach individual goals they'd set for themselves. Nothing else mattered in the moment. These athletes were so determined, so motivated, so exuberant in pursuit of their goals that I could tangibly feel the collective force and power of their ambition. The word that came to mind, that best described what I was watching, was *aspiration*.

It came down to dreams and goals. Not idle dreams or fuzzy goals, but hard, fast targets to aim for. *That* is what pulled these fighters out of the darkness and into the arena, where they now demonstrated such vitality. That was where I, the injured journalist, intersected with these injured soldiers—at the exact point of their propulsive aspirations.

Having a clear, fixed goal is what saved me. From the moment I regained consciousness in bombed-out Horenka, I had a goal—to somehow and at any cost make it back to my family. That goal, that aspiration, gave me the fortitude I needed to make it out of Ukraine alive, to get through months and months of painful rehab, and, finally, to be reunited with Alicia and the girls.

All the athletes I interviewed told me the same thing: having a goal, having a dream, is what pulled them through their most difficult times. The goal was the engine, the driving force, behind all the effort and momentum that was needed. The goal was *essential* to their recovery. Their journeys to achieve those goals, however, were not great leaps but rather a series of tiny steps. Steps so small and granular that sometimes their goals seemed out of reach. But, like me, they came to realize that each tiny step brought them closer to the top of the ladder. Each rung gave them a better view of their horizon.

The driving force we so desperately need to overcome a challenge can be just about anything. You find it by asking: *What matters most to me in the world? What am I willing to fight the hardest for?* There is no one answer to these questions: all answers are correct. We embrace what we desire, and we fight for what we love.

Yet the act of having and chasing a goal was not quite all I was witnessing in Merkur Spiel-Arena. There was something else, something bigger and deeper.

My goal was to get back to my family—to play with my daughters, walk my beloved dog, sit around and talk at dinner, be with Alicia again. But as I sat in the stands, I realized something about the goals we all set. I realized their true power lies not in setting them, but in constantly *resetting* them.

I had already learned on my journey that "getting back to normal" is not quite enough of a goal. I know that sounds contradictory because I just wrote that getting back to my "normal" domestic routine *was* my goal. But in retrospect, I can see that it wasn't *just* getting back to normal. What really and truly motivated me was returning to my family *as a better human being*. A better father, a better husband, a better friend and colleague, more in tune with my real priorities, more authentically me. Only now can I see that what happened to me was a singular opportunity to not just get back to the way I was, but to grow and change into someone bigger and better. To *aspire*.

Aspiration is defined not just as chasing a goal, but as "a strong desire to achieve something *high or great*." To aspire is to dream bigger and fight harder than we may have thought was possible. Overcoming the challenges we face will inevitably surface strengths and abilities we've never tapped into before, and to not use these new powers to push ourselves toward higher and greater things is to set artificial limits on ourselves and leave our ultimate potential unexplored.

The athletes I watched at the Invictus Games refused to do that. They may have started simply by wanting to get back to normal, but what truly drove them was a desire to *triumph*. To test themselves and push their limits and compete and excel and ultimately to be the best at something. To rise up into their truest and most capable selves. It is okay to start out with small goals, but I didn't want to stop there. Once I've achieved something, I quickly set another goal. I aim even higher. I believe in my ability to succeed at whatever I do. When we evolve our goals—from small to big, from simple to complex—we evolve our minds, and that is how we grow as humans. That is how we reach our highest potential.

And *that*, I realized, was the real story I was covering.

The story wasn't about disabled people.

The story was about *resilient* people.

*   *   *

Long after I returned to London from the Games, and after I'd filmed several reports about them that aired on Fox News, some of the thoughts I had during Invictus stayed with me.

I thought a lot about overcoming the perceptions that hold us back—the artificial limits we put on ourselves. I thought about how we truly are all capable of breaking through ceilings and tearing down walls and finding the space to thrive. Prince Harry got it right during his speech, saying, "Claim this experience. Claim this moment. Grasp every opportunity and revel in it. Because in your joy, in your happiness, in your achievement, we all benefit."

And I thought again about the phrase that best describes the higher purpose we should all aspire to uncover:

The *limitless* in us.

I finally had an answer to the nagging question I'd wrestled with for so long. I'm not pretentious enough to believe I had unearthed some mystical, universal truth, but by recognizing how much control we all have in determining the outcome of our battles, I began to understand my own struggle better. It doesn't happen overnight, but when we accept that we aren't bound by the disasters that beset us, but rather are *freed* by them, we can grow and change and be better. We need to believe that residing somewhere within us all is a well of strength and power and resilience that is truly limitless.

The U.S. team at the Invictus Games adopted a motto that best expressed what they'd learned about themselves in their individual journeys of recovery and improvement. It originally came from a poem by William Ernest Henley titled "Invictus," and it was later used by Winston Churchill in a famous speech.

These brave athletes were, they proudly declared, *Masters of Our Fate*.

9

MARIINSKYI PALACE

November 18, 2023

Rzeszow Airport, Poland

Our plane touched down in the city of Rzeszow in southern Poland in the dark of night. A car was waiting and soon we were heading east on European Route 40. The shadowy border between Poland and Ukraine loomed several miles ahead, and as we got nearer, I felt a familiar sensation. A shift, a tightening, an alertness, almost a *click* into another gear. I felt it every time I got near a combat zone, and now I felt it again, for the first time in more than eighteen months.

On one side of the border was peace.

On the other, war.

I was steeling myself to cross that border.

I'd been there before—not there, exactly, but on E373, a similar road to the north, heading for the same border, feeling the same click. That was in 2022, when I first crossed into Ukraine in an old, rented station wagon, geared up with my body armor, helmet, and med pack. Russia had invaded Ukraine just days earlier, before dawn on February 24, in the largest military mobilization since World War II, and I went there to cover the conflict for Fox News. Back then the border was in perpetual chaos, as millions of women and children tried desperately to flee the country ahead of the Russian bombs. The border was quieter now, more than eighteen months later, but the war raged on. Ukraine remained under constant attack—fifty-eight air strikes just on the day I returned there.

About six months earlier, I received an invitation from Ukrainian president Volodymyr Zelenskyy to come back to the country and meet with him in the Mariinskyi Palace in Kyiv, from where he'd been orchestrating the resistance to Russia's takeover attempt. Zelenskyy knew my story—how I'd been badly injured in a bombing outside Kyiv, somehow made it out of the country, and was now recovering at home—and he believed my return to Ukraine would be symbolic of a much greater achievement. The message he wished to convey was one of resilience—the incredible resilience of the Ukrainian people and soldiers, and of the scores of journalists who risk their lives to shine a light on Russia's aggression for the world to see. Having me walk into the palace under my own power would symbolize a refusal to surrender to the odds, a resolve to keep going, to keep fighting, to persevere.

Professionally, interviewing Zelenskyy in Kyiv at a crucial moment in the war was a journalistic coup, and that alone made me want to immediately pack my bags.

But I also believed in Zelenskyy's message, and I was happy to help him deliver it. What's more, returning to Ukraine would also be a highly personal and meaningful journey, the chance to retrace the steps of my unlikely rescue eighteen months earlier, and to try to come to terms with the day when I was all but dead and gone.

*   *   *

By some reports, Russian president Vladimir Putin expected to make quick work of the Ukraine resistance to his onslaught of military might, ending the war in just three days or, at worst, announcing the annexation of Ukraine by May 9, 2022, Russia's Victory Day, ten weeks after the invasion. Things did not work out that way. As of this writing, the war has passed the two-year mark, with no feasible end in sight. In that time, perhaps the biggest story in the world has been the remarkable, enduring resilience of Zelenskyy, his country, and its soldiers and civilians.

Everywhere in the country, there are stories of uncanny resolve. In October 2022, Russian missiles cut off 80 percent of the water supply to Kyiv, the nation's capital. Somehow, utility workers defied a continuing barrage of bombings and restored the full flow of water to Kyiv in *twenty-four hours*. By that same month in 2022, Russia's ceaseless assault had significantly damaged half of Ukraine's energy infrastructure, and a full energy backout seemed inevitable. But Ukrainians scrambled and implemented emergency measures and kept the country's energy grid operational. The same attacks nearly crippled Ukraine's oil and gas infrastructure, but again Ukrainian workers established alternate supply networks, quickly deployed repair workers, and otherwise prevented a full loss of power in the country.

Also, when Russian bombs knocked out the electricity at a thermal power plant in March 2024, a worker named Ihor found a flashlight and stayed in the darkened plant as its walls crumbled, making fixes that kept the system going. "The boys on the front are defending our country," said Oleh, another plant worker, "and we are fighting here as much as we can."

Of course, Ukraine's resistance has come with a horrific cost. Casualty estimates are hard to pin down, but according to a leaked Pentagon document, at least 17,500 Ukrainians, and as many as 70,000, have been killed since the invasion (Russia's losses have been even higher). Some 200,000 buildings across the country have been destroyed; museums looted, schools and hospitals cratered by bombs, whole cities reduced to rubble. The damage in dollar terms is nearing $200 billion.

The devastation in Ukraine defies comprehension. A proud country that grew and often prospered after declaring independence in 1991 is being crushed by Russian aggression, its existence very much in question. Ukraine has had to endure an endless string of setbacks, including a failed offensive in 2023 and the U.S. Congress's long delay in sending crucial funds to the country. Nevertheless, Ukrainian resistance, and Zelenskyy's refusal to accept a peace treaty that cedes some of its land to Russia, continue unabated, a supreme display of resilience the world has rarely seen.

This was history in the making, and every part of me wanted to return to Ukraine and see it firsthand. It was something I *had* to do.

Alicia understood that, just as she understood that venturing into the war zone in Ukraine the first time, in March 2022, was something I had to do. This time, though, she set some conditions. She insisted that I not rush into the trip, and that I make sure I was healthy enough to go. And she wanted me to wait until it was the safest possible time for such a trip. In late 2023, Russia and Ukraine were locked in a kind of stalemate across the eastern part of the country, and hostilities were slowing down rather than picking up. The timing seemed right.

But just a few days before I was scheduled to leave, the fighting in Ukraine suddenly intensified, with some of the heaviest bombing since

the invasion began. On November 18, the day of my scheduled de-
parture, there were 64 combat engagements in Ukraine, with Russia
launching five missile and 58 air strikes, including 33 multiple-launch
rocket system attacks on Ukrainian troops. That night Russia continued to pound Ukrainian infrastructure facilities with Shahed-136/131
Iranian-made attack drones.

By then my trip had been fully arranged, and if I were to call it off
there was no telling when, or even if, I'd be able to do the interview.
I assured Alicia that I'd be traveling in a cocoon of tight security, and
that despite the increase in bombings I'd be as safe going now as I'd
ever be.

And so, 614 days after the attack that changed my life, I was back
in Ukraine.

On the flight from London to Poland, I still felt like this was just
any other trip for me. But once the small Fox team I was traveling with
landed at the airport in Balice, outside Kraków, and got on E40 heading to the Poland-Ukraine border, it hit me that this was no ordinary
assignment. Familiar feelings bubbled up—hunger to get the story,
alertness to the danger. It was like I'd somehow gone back in time.

We arrived at the Przemyśl Główny train station in the Polish
town of Przemyśl, nine miles from the Ukrainian border. I walked
along the platform beside a parked passenger locomotive painted
blue and yellow and destined for Kyiv. Seeing the train was surreal. I
was precisely retracing the steps of my rescue in reverse. The last time
I'd been on this train, it took three people to wrap me in an orange
hospital blanket, yank me off a gurney, and hoist my prone and broken body up the metal stairs and through the narrow doorway of one
of the train cars.

This time, I walked aboard on my own—limping, in pain, taking
one step at a time, but, still, on my own.

The last time, I was loaded in the lower right bunk in a plain sleeper compartment, where I spent the next ten hours slipping in and out of consciousness and fighting off extreme pain. This time I sat in a leather banquette seat in my own plush compartment with gold silk curtains and framed portraits of world leaders who'd been on board before, including President Biden. Back in 2022, I was essentially a stowaway on a top-secret diplomatic train, whisked on board at the last moment and stashed away. Now I was a guest of President Zelenskyy and a world-class security team. In 2022, I wore body armor at all times. Now our flak jackets followed in the baggage. The contrast between the two train rides was not lost on me.

It was late when we boarded for the overnight train journey, and after an hour or so I pulled down the sleeper bunk, which had a clean sheet and blanket on it, and tried to get some sleep. But it was no use. I couldn't sleep. The movement of the train, the steady rattling of the rail wheels on the steel tracks, was like a sensory cue that took me right back to the 2022 train ride out of Kyiv. Rather than fight it, I welcomed it. This, after all, was one of the reasons I had come—to reexperience what happened to me nearly two years earlier. I tried to lie in the very same position I'd been in on the 2022 train. I closed my eyes and narrowed my focus to memories of that night, trying to summon what it felt like to even be alive after the bombing, and to still be on death's door as we lurched through Ukraine. I tried to remember if it struck me then, as it did now, how very fragile life is, how it sometimes hangs by a thread.

I tried to recall how I could have been so positive, so certain that I'd make it home alive, in the face of such long odds that suggested otherwise.

One sensation resurfaced—the absolute chaos I felt in my mind on the first train ride. My brain was like a live wire, thrashing and firing off sparks, racing through a series of crazy, adrenalized thoughts and ideas, spiraling incessantly in different directions, all completely out of my control to stop or even slow down. This went on for *hours*, keeping me awake for most of the ride. My brain, it would seem, was broken.

Now, more than eighteen months later, I looked back on those frenzied hours and thought about the head injuries that likely caused my synapses to fire so randomly. I touched the spot on my left temple where shrapnel had struck and caused a traumatic brain injury. I thought about how close I'd come to an even worse injury. Had the shrapnel hit an inch lower, or been an ounce thicker, who knows what would have happened? Yet there I was, back on the train, this time in full control of my thoughts. *What a gift!* I thought. *How lucky am I? How precious is life?* Even though I was resurfacing memories of one of the most painful, darkest nights of my life, I now felt a profound sense of comfort. My memories weren't frightening at all; they were affirmations, and they filled me with joy and gratitude for whatever it was inside me that allowed me to survive and persevere and keep going after the bombing.

The train rattled on, the noisy forward movement evocative of life itself, and I kept my eyes closed and stayed in the past. I thought about my beloved colleague Pierre Zakrzewski, the Fox News cameraman who had been in the car with me in Horenka when the bombs struck, and about the young Ukrainian journalist, Oleksandra Kuvshynova, whom we called Sasha, and who had been in the car too. Sasha, just twenty-four, signed on to be our fixer so she could help spread the word about what was happening in her beloved country. Pierre, like me, was a journalist to his bones, and together we'd covered many wars and much tragedy, and we'd become far more than just colleagues—we were brothers.

I thought back to the moments after the bombings. I remembered the intense heat as I rolled on the ground, trying to smother the flames. I remembered looking down at my nearly severed leg and reaching for my cell phone to take a picture of it. I remembered looking past my leg and seeing Pierre lying on the ground farther down the slope, motionless. I remembered calling to him and hearing him respond. I remembered being on the train when I was told that Pierre and Sasha had died. Back then I was in too much pain and too foggy-headed to be able to contemplate their deaths, but on the second train ride, in my comfortable compartment, I felt a wave of fresh emotion.

And I found myself talking to Pierre.

Pierre, good friend, I know you'd be so happy to see me going back. I know you'd be going back with me if you could. I am here now, doing this, with you very much in mind, old friend. This is not just for me, it's for us. We are showing them that they can never stop the beautiful dream we had—the dream that the world is a wonderful place filled with miraculous people, that life is beautiful and worth fighting for, and that as long as we keep shining a light on the horrors of war, goodness will always prevail.

Rest well, good friend. Soon we'll be in Kyiv.

It was daybreak when we finally reached the capital, and the sun was shining, and under my own power I walked off that locomotive and onto the platform, and I felt strong—stronger than I had at any time since the bombing—as if I'd made it through that terrible night all over again, and was better off because of it, and could now confront any challenge, and keep going, keep pushing, until I made it through.

* · * · *

In Kyiv, President Zelenskyy's security detail hurried our small Fox News team in SUVs to our hotel, the InterContinental, not far from Mariinskyi Palace. The day was tightly scheduled, and I had a half hour at the hotel to get ready to attend various events leading up to my interview with Zelenskyy. I took the time to call Alicia in London.

Alicia was the underlying reason I decided to return to Ukraine. In fact, she was the foundational factor behind every decision I now made. What got me through the escape from Ukraine and my rehab in Texas was the thought of getting back home to Alicia and the girls. If she wasn't physically with me in Kyiv, she was with me spiritually, as crucial a part of the experience as anything or anyone else. Everything I did was for her, for us. My journey wasn't a solo journey—Alicia and I were on it together, and every victory, every setback, was ours together, and any psychological milestone along the way, like returning to the place where I nearly died, was a milestone for both of us, for our family, to achieve together.

I reached Alicia at home and told her everything was fine. On the phone she sounded perfectly calm, but she later told me she was anxious the whole time I was on the ground in Ukraine. It was true that I was in a war zone, and that I could occasionally hear the sirens warning of bomb attacks in the distance. But as I told Alicia again on the phone that morning, I was traveling inside an extremely tight security bubble and I was as safe as I possibly could be in Kyiv. Soon I would be with President Zelenskyy, and she didn't need to worry about me then. I'd be in good hands.

Alicia understood all that, but she worried anyway.

I had to keep the phone call brief. I told Alicia I loved her and would call her after the interview (my phone would be confiscated while I was with Zelenskyy). I said I'd be home soon, and I asked her to kiss the girls for me. Then security officials arrived to take me to the War Memorial in Kyiv, where I laid flowers and said a prayer over the thousands of photos of civilian victims posted around the memorial. From there we traveled to St. Volodymyr's Cathedral, in the center of Kyiv. The mother cathedral of the Ukrainian Orthodox Church, it is an astonishing neo-Byzantine monument, a six-piered, three-apsed temple with seven glorious cupolas and a brilliantly bright yellow façade. The main dome features a 161-foot cross set against its guided walls and vaunted rises. We sat with fifteen religious leaders from around the country and talked about how religion was being used as a weapon in the war.

As I stood in the church, I thought again of Pierre.

He was just a brilliant human being. Known as much for his exuberant mustache as for his generous, loving spirit, Pierre cherished traveling the world and meeting new people. He could befriend just about anyone (including enemy rebels), and he saw it as his purpose to spread good wherever he went. Pierre stood for uniting cultures, telling people in one corner of the world about people he met in another, shrinking the planet as best he could. In that church, I wanted more than anything to have Pierre live on through me. I wanted my presence there to stand for both of us, to be a continuation of his call for a more beautiful world. Mostly, I wanted Pierre to know that the awe and inspiration I felt in that church was his as well as mine, and that I would travel the world for both of us, keeping his passions alive—keeping *him* alive.

This was my little prayer for Pierre in that magnificent cathedral. I wanted him to know he was still with us.

Next I was taken to Mariinskyi Palace, the official residence of the president of Ukraine. The palace is a vast, commanding structure:

a baroque, Elizabethan architectural marvel, built by the Russian empress Elizaveta Petrovna in 1744, then rebuilt after a fire by Emperor Alexander II in 1870. From the outside, it looks pristine and stately. But inside, there were signs of war everywhere. Most of the lights were turned off, an effort to conserve power. We walked down a long, dark, cold corridor that had sandbags set up in front of the windows and at intervals on the floor, like little checkpoints, meant to slow Russian invaders should they get inside the palace. We made it upstairs and arrived at a room with bright lights on, done up in the typical glitz and glamour of Eastern European political elites—a massive round table, several national flags, plush gold curtains. Finally, we were ushered into the president's private office.

I was in a suit jacket, but not dress pants. As I always did when I traveled, I wore knee-length shorts that revealed my sleek-looking prosthetics. It was a deliberate decision not to hide what had happened to me (my blue sneakers weren't a statement, they were for comfort). The president soon entered, and he walked over and we shook hands. His grip was firm and full. He was in his familiar green military pants and black long-sleeved sweater, an outfit befitting a wartime president.

Zelenskyy's words—broken English in a deep voice—echoed through the room. Here was a world leader who in a time of war had brought his country together and held it together in a remarkable, historic act of defiance. I'd met world leaders before, but Zelenskyy, who was literally fighting for his life and the lives of his people when we met, struck me as a truly fascinating figure. He very graciously presented me with a medal, known as Ukraine's Order of Merit, III Class, in honor of my "outstanding personal contribution to strengthening interstate cooperation, support for Ukraine's independence and territorial integrity." The medal, of course, was not just for me. It was for Pierre and Sasha, and the more than seventy journalists who had lost their lives during the war, and indeed for all the hundreds of journalists who risk their lives every day to cover the war in Ukraine, and everywhere around the world.

"All this time, journalists, cameramen, editors, photographers, drivers have been on the front line," Zelenskyy said. "As this is a hybrid war, information is also a weapon in Russian hands. My sincere condolences to the families and friends of those very brave men and women who lost their lives trying to show what is happening in Ukraine. In particular, it is thanks to journalists from many countries that we now have such support in the world."

We were led to a long wooden conference table for a debriefing about the war, with Zelenskyy at the head of the table and other government officials seated around us. Then the president and I moved to an area where cameras had been set up to capture our interview. In general, Zelenskyy did not grant many in-depth interviews. But we spoke for ninety minutes, and we didn't waste any of them—I jumped right in and asked about the precarious state of Ukraine's resistance, and about how the world's attention had been shifted away by the horrific Hamas attack in Israel.

"Yes, you are right, it doesn't have a good influence on Ukraine," Zelenskyy said of the shifted focus. "It doesn't help us. But we understand there is also a challenge for the world in the Middle East." Sowing chaos all over the world through allies like Iran, he added, "was a really big wish for Russia."

At the same time, after a year of unquestioned financial and military support from the United States to Ukraine, Republicans in the U.S. were fighting to stop the flow of funds, arguing that the money should be spent at home. "I hope that the help of United States will be around Ukrainian people," Zelenskyy said. "I hope the United

States will be with us against Russian terrorism. We are fighting for [the] Commonwealth, it's very important. But we are losing *our* people, we're not losing Europeans or Americans."

Zelenskyy's point was that the battle to save Ukraine was a battle to prevent a much larger war, in which the casualties would not be limited to Ukrainians. In recent months Russia had made significant tactical advances around Kharkiv, Ukraine's second-largest city, and had already seized huge swaths of land in the Donbas region to the east, and also in the south, and this was where Zelenskyy faced his hardest fights. But just as important was his fight to swing the world's attention back to Ukraine, and to convince skeptical Republicans in Congress that investing in Ukraine was investing in a peaceful future for Europe, and the world.

"Ukraine today is in the center of these global risks of a third world war," Zelenskyy forcefully told me. "And I really think that Russia will push and push until the United States and China together will tell them to go out of the territory. If Russia won't go out, it means that politically, in the world, we all lose. It means Russia won't be afraid of [Western military] power. This is not a good message."

I sensed that behind his words and pronouncements there was a slight trace of desperation, perhaps even disillusionment, because of how Ukraine had fallen out of the world's sharp focus. I felt he was basically calling out the world, imploring them to see what he was seeing—to understand how tenuous his grasp on the country was. It was almost like he was pleading, *People of the world, we really need your help, or else we are going to be beaten*—which was essentially the assessment of most war analysts at that time. Still, that was all subtext that I perceived. His words, his demeanor, were defiant, especially when he declared his intention to never surrender his country to Russia. At that time, certain politicians in the U.S. were floating ideas for a peace plan that called for Zelenskyy to cede much, if not all, of the land taken by Russia in exchange for a cease-fire. When I asked him if he would be amenable to such a plan, he was decisive, striking a harsher, more defiant tone that he had in recent months.

"Yes, we can stop this war if we will give Russia Donbas and Crimea," Zelenskyy said. "But in my mind our country will not be ready for such a peace plan. To me, that is not a peace plan at all."

When I could, I brought up Pierre and Sasha. I asked Zelenskyy if he had a message for their families and loved ones, who, like me, were still struggling with their loss.

"These very brave guys and woman lost their lives because they really wanted to help Ukraine to be alive," he said. "We can't give them back to you, your sons and daughters. But we will never, ever forget them."

When we finished the interview, I realized that our entire discussion had been about one thing—what it meant to be resilient in today's dangerous world.

The Ukrainians were badly outmatched by the Russians—by some estimates, Russia had three times as many soldiers, and far superior military weaponry—yet, more than two years into what was expected to a three-week conflict, Ukraine had not been defeated. Nor had it been bowed. The last two winters had been hellish tests of endurance for Ukrainians, with energy supplies low and Russian attacks continuing. But the country had survived its long winters and still remained defiant, unwilling to cede an inch to the militarily superior Russian forces—which, at the hands of Ukraine's surprisingly nimble counteroffensive, had suffered the loss of many tens of thousands of its own soldiers, and billions in military equipment. The only real explanation for Ukraine's historic defiance was the iron will of its people.

"War, victory, defeat, stagnation depend on many decisions, many risks, many areas," Zelenskyy believes. "But mostly, it all depends on us. If we preserve our resilience, we will end the war."

When our interview concluded, I had a bit of time to pursue a personal goal. Originally, what I'd hoped for most of all was the chance to return to the village of Horenka, where the Russian bombs had struck our car and killed four of the five people in it. I wanted to go back to the very spot where I woke up after the third missile struck, gravely injured but still alive. I wanted to stand where I had lain, so I could see and feel it all again, and remember details I'd forgotten, and draw strength from the fact that I'd returned. I wanted to honor Pierre and Sasha there, and talk to Pierre, and let him know I'd made it back—that we'd *both* made it back.

When I shared this wish with others, though, most people couldn't understand why I would want to go back to a place where I almost died. Of course, I saw it differently. For me, returning to Horenka was a pilgrimage of sorts, part of a spiritual journey. Being there again, in that spot, would be a meaningful, psychological triumph, a declaration that no matter what the world threw at me, I would not be stopped, I would not be defeated.

I would not be defined by what happened to me in that village. No—I would be defined by the way I've reacted to it.

Unfortunately, returning to Horenka wasn't possible given our tight schedule and the security measures it would require. Instead I went to meet the people who had rescued me, at the National Military Medical Center, on Hospitalna Street in Kyiv, not far from the banks of the Dnipro River. It was there that our security consultant, Jock, finally located me after hours of scouring local hospitals. Jock texted Fox News reporter Trey Yingst, my colleague in Ukraine, to let him know I'd been found, banged up but alive. *Ben is currently undergoing serious operations*, he texted. *Fracture to base of skull. Left eye cut in half. Brain op at 2:30, two pieces of shrapnel from skull. An op to save his left foot.*

All I remember of the hospital was waking up in a clean bed in a large room and seeing metal rods sticking out of my right thigh. I remembered seeing a man in a hospital bed across from me, and immediately taking him for an armed Russian operative (I was a bit addled by painkillers). Not much later, my rescuers—Rich Jadick, Bo, and Seaspray—wheeled me out of the hospital and put me into a rickety old ambulance they'd recently purchased from the backyard of a junk dealer by the Baltic Sea. The ambulance was cramped and couldn't go any faster than 15 miles per hour. As I mentioned earlier, my Ukrainian doctor urged our team not to take me, for fear that movement might dislodge the shrapnel in my throat.

But the doctor also admitted he was equally worried about having me stay at the hospital in Kyiv, which the Russians could bomb at any moment. No one was interested in having an American journalist die under their care.

In the end, the doctor agreed to let me go with Jadick, Bo, and Seaspray, who assured him they had a plan to move me out of Ukraine in the smoothest, least disruptive way possible. Immediately after seeing us off, the doctor grabbed his rifle and set off for his post. He was a highly skilled surgeon, but he was a Ukrainian first, and like every able-bodied man he didn't hesitate to take up arms and fight for his country.

More than eighteen months later, when I met the same doctor outside the same hospital, he could not believe I was still alive.

"My God, you were *gone*," he said through tears. "You shouldn't be here. It is a miracle you are here."

It was a deeply emotional moment for us both. Of course, he was right—I *shouldn't* have been there. The last time he laid eyes on me, the chances of my survival were slim. I was one day removed from an amputation. I was bleeding from several places. I had no access to the care or medication I would need to survive, or at least I wouldn't for several crucial hours, if at all. I was, in effect, closer to dying than living.

Yet I made it. And now I was back, standing before the doctor, flesh and blood and a little machinery, relatively healthy and smiling. Reborn, in a way. Raised from the dead. A miracle, as the doctor put it.

I shook the doctor's hand, and we held each other's grip for a long moment. I'd thought about what I would say to him, but when we met I simply spoke from the heart. "From my family," I said, "from my children and my wife, we all want to say thank you, *thank you*, for getting me home to them. My family will forever be grateful to you."

Then we hugged, both of us blessed and grateful to be there, for what it said about us that he had helped me survive and that I'd made it all the way back, but also for what it said about Ukraine, and about the human spirit.

*   *   *

By the next evening, I was back in London with Alicia and the girls. My trip to Ukraine had been short but intense. I had a lot of feelings to sort through, but I think I accomplished what I set out to do. Before I left on this trip, some people asked, *Why are you going back? You almost died there, and it's still a war zone. You made it out alive and made it all the way back to your family, and now you want to put yourself at risk again? Isn't that selfish of you?*

I understood their point, but I just didn't see it that way. Before my return trip to Ukraine, Alicia and I talked an awful lot about me going. By then she already knew that I wanted to go back, not because I told her, but because she knew *me*. She respected that this was the way I was built. She could have insisted I not go, but she'd never stopped me from following my gut instincts before, and she wasn't going to start now, not even after what happened in Horenka. Still, we talked at length about what would need to happen before I could return to Ukraine, and I followed her suggestions and waited several months until I was healthier and the perfect opportunity to travel safely turned up. Had I believed I was truly putting myself in real danger, I would not have gone.

Of course, as Alicia has reminded me, I'm not always the best judge of what *danger* means.

Alicia understood that I needed to *not* be hesitant to go back. I could not take what happened to me and stuff it away and try to forget it. My return to Ukraine was about *confronting* everything that happened to me that day, thinking about it, talking about it, processing it as best I could. It was about proving to myself that the injuries I suffered were *not* going to stop me. For me, the trip was part of an ongoing physical, mental, and spiritual recovery. I needed to go back. I needed to feel it all again.

I needed to come full circle.

That was a lot to ask of such a short trip, but in the end I was not disappointed. I came back feeling stronger than I had since the bombings. I felt more capable, more resilient, *because* I'd gone back and faced it all again.

Then there was President Zelenskyy. My interview with him was one of the highlights of my career as a journalist, but it was his personal fortitude that stood out for me, and inspires me as I wage my own far, far smaller battle against the odds. In my journey, I've learned so much about accepting and embracing challenges, about aspiring to better myself through them, and about resisting the pitfalls that come with them. Along with all that, I learned there is something else I can do as I strive to overcome obstacles—I can *defy* expectations.

This means building a mindset that refuses to accept conventional thinking and popular opinion and instead drives me to *defy* predictions for my success.

It was only a few days after the bombing that I first set the goal of returning to Ukraine, a goal that at the time defied all logic. Well, *so what* if it defied logic? *So what* if I focused on my own goals and expectations rather than on someone else's? What if I made defiance one of the central planks of my recovery, and strived to defy logic at every step? Wouldn't that give me more strength and inspiration than accepting limitations other people imposed on me?

So much of how we confront challenges is mental, and adopting a defiant mindset is one way we can change the way we see and react to obstacles. My return to Ukraine proved to me that I have what it takes to rise above setbacks and persevere and, ultimately, defy expectations.

Early on after I made it home to London in 2022, my daughters Honor, Iris, and Hero, then six, four, and two years old, would occasionally say things like, "You're not going back there, Daddy, are you? You're never going back, right?" I assured them I had no plans to return to Ukraine anytime soon. They were so young, and what could they possibly have understood of war and bombs and death? All they knew was that the place where I'd been injured was a terrible one.

At the same time, the girls had likely spent more time thinking about what it means to be at war than most children their age. They understood what I did for a living, and they had a general sense of the eternal battle between right and wrong. Whenever they asked me questions about Ukraine or the bombing, I was careful to shield them from the harsher realities of conflict, but I didn't want to completely whitewash what was happening in other countries. "Yes, it is an awful place right now," I'd say, "but it is also a very beautiful place, and the good guys can make it safe to be there again."

The point I was trying to make with my smart-beyond-their-years daughters was that we can't just turn our backs on what is happening in the world. We are all part of a global community, and we all must do what we can to make it a better place. Both Alicia and I welcomed these little talks with our daughters; we both want them to grow up to be thoughtful, caring women guided by conscience and morals. We don't want them to ever turn their backs on the problems of the world.

That, perhaps, is the main reason I chose to return to Ukraine. Because being defiant in the face of overwhelming odds gives you a kind of superhuman strength to surpass your goals and discover who you truly are inside.

10

SECRET WEAPON

May 2024

West London, England

Our Lab, Bosco, woke us up with loud barking. It was one in the morning. Bosco sometimes barked at noises in the middle of the night, but this time he was in a fit, and Alicia and I were instantly up in our beds on the second floor. My instinct was to jump up and dash downstairs and see what the hell was happening.

But I can't jump or dash anymore.

So, Alicia, who at the time was pregnant, did. She came down the stairs and ran into the living room and saw three men forcing their way through a window. One of them was halfway into the house. From upstairs I heard Alicia scream, *Get out!* as I hurriedly strapped on my prosthetics. By the time I made it downstairs, Alicia and Bosco had chased the burglars away.

"I think they were more terrified of me than I was of them," Alicia says now. "They woke me up, and I don't like being woken up."

The burglars had managed to stealthily break the locks on an outer and inner window and were climbing through into the living room when they knocked against a table, rousing Bosco and then us. Ironically, just a few weeks earlier, Alicia and I had been awakened by a strange noise downstairs, and again it was Alicia, not me, who raced down to see what it was. No one was there then, but it proved a dry run for the night the burglars did appear. We called the police, who promptly arrived and turned up the next day as well to collect fingerprints. Luckily, our two youngest daughters slept through the racket, but our eldest, Honor, straggled downstairs to see what the fuss was about. Alicia and I didn't lie to her; we told her what happened, and that we were safe now, everything was fine. She was a bit spooked, as were we, but by the next day she was happily helping the forensic expert dust for prints on our window.

That frightening night was an eye-opener. For one thing, neither of us knew if Bosco was the type of dog to play guard and bark at intruders, or the type to curl up under a table and watch the thieves at work. He'd never been tested before, and I was proud to see that he more than rose to the occasion, barking madly until the thieves were gone and, for good measure, long after.

Even more eye-opening was how Alicia and I, without ever discussing it, instinctively switched roles.

I was supposed to be the man of the house, the one who grabs a golf club or cricket bat (or in my case, a tribal baton I picked up in Kenya) and chases off the burglars while his wife stays with the girls upstairs. "That was the unspoken agreement," Alicia said when we sat down later and reflected on what happened. "In the past I wouldn't have even followed you downstairs, I would have huddled with the girls to make sure they were okay and to be there in case I had to get them somewhere safe. That would have been my instinct. Whereas with you, even that night, your instinct was to follow me downstairs rather than stay with the girls."

Of course, I understood intellectually that things had changed for Alicia and me, and that there were many roles I'd no longer be able to play. I slept without my prosthetics on, and while I'd shortened the length of time it took me to strap them on, it was by no means a quick process. I understood and accepted that. It was our new reality.

Even so, it was a shock to see Alicia, without hesitation, race ahead of me downstairs and scare off the burglars. She even had the presence of mind to take her cell phone with her downstairs, and she called the police before I had a chance to. Contrary to my every instinct, I've had to accept that our new reality means that, sometimes, it will be Alicia and not me who steps up to be the family's protector.

The truth, however, is that—my wounded male pride aside—I've always known Alicia has been our family's protector, not just during break-ins, but every hour of every day. For all the lessons I've learned since I was injured in Ukraine, my wellness and recovery have benefited most from what you might call a secret weapon.

My secret weapon is Alicia.

*　　　*　　　*

I remember something my friend Sarah Verardo once said about her husband, Michael, after he was injured in Afghanistan and had to rely on her to get him through the dark moments of his slow recovery. When I spoke with Sarah about the role she played for Michael, she said, "I do not take it lightly that I'm the person Michael trusts to make the decisions that are best for him and for our girls and for our whole family. He has a faith in me that I will work every day to fully deserve that trust.

"Michael," she concluded, "knows I am his person."

In the same way, I know Alicia is my person.

Not long ago, Alicia and I sat at the slatted wood table in our garden on an overcast day and talked about everything we've been through over the last two years.

I wanted to root around for more insight into her quiet heroism— and I wanted to thank her for all the times she was there to pick me up when I fell. Alicia played a part in getting me home even *before* she knew I was injured. Moments after the third missile struck, when I woke up on the ground and on fire, I felt Alicia and the girls were with me, willing me to safety. I felt an overwhelming determination to get back to Alicia and the girls, and this determination was far, far more powerful than fear or logic or desperation or anything else I might have felt.

Alicia was right there with me even when she *wasn't* right there with me.

From that moment onward, Alicia was my guide. When she learned I'd been injured, she kept her cool and immediately took charge of the decision-making for our family, starting with giving her okay for the risky operation to move me out of Ukraine, which would not have happened without her approval. "I knew there were only two options: stay or move," Alicia told me. "And I knew you are a mover. You never want to stay put. You always want to go."

Together, Alicia and I agreed it would be best for the girls if she remained in London with them while I rehabbed in Texas, rather than yanking them out of school and bringing them to the States. But that meant Alicia would have to handle everything—meals, schedules, bedtimes, bills, ballet recitals, netball matches, on top of the emotional state of our daughters and herself—almost entirely on her own.

Once again, without hesitation, she threw herself into the task and maintained a remarkable amount of normalcy and stability for the girls in a situation that was anything but stable. Alicia made the very smart decision to shield the girls from the madness of those first few weeks, telling them only that I had been hurt in an accident and would be away for a while recovering—and making sure no teachers or parents of classmates told them any more than that. Then, over time, Alicia eased Hero, Iris, and Honor into the reality of their father coming home with a prosthetic leg—or, as they referred to it, a robot leg. I'm still in awe of how Alicia maintained a household, dealt with my doctors, paid all the bills, planned for my return, shepherded the girls through a dark time, *and* somehow took care of herself and handled her own emotions so that the girls never saw whatever fear or anxiety she felt.

Even when I made it home to London, this lopsided division of labor persisted. "Basically, we were living in two separate areas of the house," Alicia said in our talk. "You were all the way upstairs, working on everything you needed to work on, and I was all the way downstairs busy with the kids, having them in the house, getting them ready for school, taking them to school. There was a gap from seven a.m. to ten a.m. when I simply could not help you, and you couldn't help me."

Alicia's uncommon fortitude comes in part from her upbringing. The daughter of Kim, an Australian father, and Scarlett, a British mother who jointly ran a global shoe company called Senso, Alicia watched her parents combine to manage both a business and a family *as a team*. Seeing how her parents split duties and complemented each other helped prepare Alicia for the unexpected turn our family took. Since she'd been part of a family business, she had no preconceived illusions that the job was nine-to-five. She understood it was 24/7. She knew problems would likely pop up at all hours, and she knew that the responsibility of fixing them rested on her shoulders. Because of that, Alicia developed a work ethic that rivals that of anyone else I know.

She proved her mettle by holding our family together in my absence, but the hardest time for both of us, we agreed, was when I came back and had to adjust to my new world. Like me, Alicia just didn't know what that world would look like.

The first big sacrifice she had to make was giving up the house we called home. She recalled an incident that happened early on in my return, when I was up in the third-floor bathroom by myself while she was getting the girls ready for school downstairs in the kitchen basement. I had neglected to bring my cell phone with me, and when I knocked my leg against the tub and started bleeding heavily, I couldn't reach my bandage or otherwise stop the bleeding. I called out for help at the top of my lungs, but Alicia could not hear me downstairs. It was around then that we both realized we would have to move to a more accommodating house.

Typically, Alicia turned the potentially chaotic uprooting of our entire lives into something positive. She took the opportunity to let go of a lot of material things we really didn't need, and this helped both of us understand that we weren't just moving, we were starting a new life together. That became the prevalent theme of our lives now—that if we all do something or go somewhere together, as a family, we are going to be fine. There is simply no pulling apart our family.

Alicia and I spoke about the early months of my recovery, when my mobility was very limited and I wasn't yet able to drive (I was still a long way from being able to navigate a specially fitted car). I needed help getting anywhere—appointments, doctor visits, a meeting two blocks away. Before the bombing, I probably did 80 percent of the driving for our family. In the months after I made it back home, it flipped to Alicia driving us 100 percent of the time.

Alicia knew how determined I was to change that. After a year of getting stronger and surer on my feet, I finally learned how to drive a custom-made car outfitted with hand controls. These controls are basically push-and-pull levers that allow you to work the gas and brake with one hand, while steering with the other. It was a bit tricky learning how to drive without using my feet at all, and it took me a couple of months to get it down, but once I had the hang of it, I have to say I really enjoyed it. Driving with your hands is a bit like a video game come to life.

Regaining the freedom and independence that driving gave me was monumental. Before the incident, I had always loved driving through new cities and countries and even around London. There's nothing quite like getting in a car and feeling the absolute freedom it gives you to go anywhere and do anything. When we finally bought a specially equipped car and I learned how to operate it, I was practically giddy with excitement. Some days, I would get in the car five or six times just to drive around, even if I didn't have anywhere to go. Driving myself meant there was one less thing I had to depend on someone else for—and it meant taking a small part of the load off Alicia.

Not all rituals, sadly, could be saved. Alicia pointed out that I had taught Honor and Iris how to ride a bicycle, but I wouldn't be able to teach Hero, our youngest, because I wouldn't be able to run alongside her. That was a bit of a stab for me, for sure. In the old days I would always spring out of bed to get Alicia a cup of tea or drink of water, and I could no longer do that either. It simply took too long to strap on my prosthetics and make my way to the kitchen, when Alicia could dash down and be back in a minute. There was also the pleasure

of Alicia and I walking the children to school together in the morning. We still do that from time to time, but now the children are on
their scooters and Alicia is chasing after them and I often find myself
twenty or thirty paces back. Not in a million years would I ever tell
the girls to slow down; I'd much rather watch them be their swift,
energetic selves. So I trail along and catch up when I can.

The key is making adjustments and being thankful for what you
still get to do. Before my injuries, Alicia and I used to love going on
long walks together. Obviously, we couldn't do that anymore. Yet
neither of us wanted to give up the ritual altogether. So now, Alicia
walks on her own and I get in my car and we meet up at the end of
the walk so I can give her a lift home. It's not the same, but in a way,
it *is* the same—it's the two of us doing something we love together.

*   *   *

In the months after returning home, Alicia and I fell into a rhythm
where I would constantly seek to expand my limits, and she would
be the voice of reason. That was pretty much our rhythm *before* I was
injured, but now I needed her wisdom and counsel more than ever.
Also, I think, I was more open to receiving it than in my younger
days, when pushing limits was a way of life for me.

One thing Alicia and I both knew I wouldn't want to give up was
my work as a journalist. These days, we sit down and talk about my
reporting trips more thoroughly than we did before the bombing;
Alicia's insight about keeping me as safe as possible, for instance,
shaped my trip to Ukraine.

I asked Alicia how the dynamic between us, as it related to my
work as a journalist, had changed since the bombing. She told me she
didn't think it *had* changed. I was still intent on telling the story of

what was happening in the world, and Alicia said she was proud of me for that. At the same time, I was aware that things were different now, and I'd been able to draw a line between the old me and the new me. Alicia noticed that and was happy I'd been able to do that, while also acknowledging that I would continue to be independent in my work, as I always had been.

From what I've noticed, Alicia has also become more aware of and versed in global conflicts and tragedies than she was before my injuries. Because of what happened to me, I suppose, certain events take on more meaning for her. After the Hamas attack on Israel on October 7, 2023, Alicia was visibly distraught over the plight of the surviving victims. After watching the initial reports about the invasion on TV, she turned to me and said, "I hope they have family around them. I hope they're okay. What can we do? How can we help them?" She is more aware of how quickly and shockingly tragedy can strike, and more aware, also, of how hard it is for people and families to get through traumatic, catastrophic events. I think she understands the importance of aggressive journalism in war-torn areas a little better than she used to, and I think that is among the reasons she gave me her blessing to go to Ukraine, where conflict and suffering seem to never let up.

So many things about Alicia impress and dazzle me, but lately it's been her great capacity for gratitude. She could have let what happened to me shut her off from ever feeling blessed or lucky, yet she constantly sees and nourishes the good in our lives. For instance, it was not lost on Alicia that in my first few months home, things were quite difficult, but that over time, as my mind sharpened and my movements quickened, things got easier. Not easy, but easier. Alicia did not take that for granted. She was probably more grateful for it than I was, given my impatient nature and desire to speed things up.

Alicia never measures our new way of life against our old one. As she explained in the garden while pouring one last cup of breakfast tea with a drop of honey and powdered milk, "It's not helpful or positive for me to say 'Oh, this is awful, I can't cope with this' or 'I really miss our wonderful old life' when the reality is there's not much choice but to keep going forward." Alicia told me she sometimes thought about all the other possible scenarios that *could* have played out for me in Ukraine instead of the one that did, and that makes her feel nothing *but* gratitude, since I made it back home to her. "I mean, I know not every family has someone who gets blown up by missiles, but there are a hundred other tragedies that can happen to anyone," she said. "It's not like I look at alternative outcomes and wish they'd happened, because I wouldn't want any other alternative. What happened to us could have been worse. Much worse. We have you back, and I am *incredibly* grateful for that."

We both agreed that sometimes tragedies have hidden blessings, among them the chance to put your life into perspective.

"I genuinely believe we haven't lost anything as a family because of what happened to you," Alicia told me—a sentiment that nearly made me tear up. "In fact, it's made us all much closer. It's given us a unified purpose. In a weird way, by going through something like that you kind of earn your stripes as a family."

* * *

Evening fell in the garden as the girls threw themselves into cartwheels and Alicia and I wrapped up our conversation, a sort of State of the Family. Our talk only made me feel more genuinely in awe of her. The way I see it, Alicia's courage and fortitude far, far exceed my own. To be able to parent through tragedy and grief and uncertainty is a feat of immense bravery, and the way Alicia kept our family together in my absence—and even today—is as awesome an achievement as I've ever witnessed. Mothers, someone once told me, set the temperature in families, and this was certainly true of Alicia. Without her there would be no insights about resilience for me to share. She is, as I said, my secret weapon. I truly believe that looking at the world the way Alicia does would greatly benefit anyone anywhere who has to face adversity.

"Each of our lives is a story," she said near the end of our talk. "Of all the things that could have happened to me in my story, I would never have envisioned what happened happening, but it did. But that is just our story. You going back to Ukraine was part of your story. The way you left there, on a stretcher, going back on your terms was the natural cycle of what needed to happen. You needed to show adversity hadn't defeated you. Life is a journey, and it's not always for the fainthearted, and it's always a work in progress. Life is hard, and you have to work really hard at it. It doesn't even matter how well you end up, but if you're not really trying, if you're not working your hardest, that's just not good enough. Life resumes, life keeps moving, and you have to find a way to keep up. But that is all part of your story, just like all of this is part of ours."

11

NIR OZ

Spring 2024
NIR OZ KIBBUTZ
Southern Israel, near the Gaza border

The first missiles launched at 6:30 a.m. on October 7, 2023, before most people were awake. Loud, droning sirens followed, and the cutting sounds of automatic gunfire. At the Nir Oz Kibbutz, an idyllic, gardened community of four hundred Israelis about two miles from the Gaza border, the breach happened at 7 a.m., when two cars raced up to the entrance gate. Two men jumped out, bombed the gate, and sprayed the security office with bullets. Dozens of men followed in. It was around then that some residents of Nir Oz got on their group WhatsApp chat and texted each other about the unfolding horror.

There are terrorists inside the Kibbutz.

Shooting in our neighborhood.

Our house is on fire. Help.

For the next twelve hellish hours, some twenty communities in southern Israel were stormed and mostly destroyed by Hamas terrorists from Gaza, in one of the ghastliest, most shocking assaults in the brutal history of the Middle East.

In what amounted to a surprise attack, at least for Israeli citizens, as many as three thousand Palestinian members of Hamas, the terrorist group that governs most of the Israeli-occupied Gaza Strip, flooded southern Israel on foot, on motorbikes, and by hang glider. They ransacked, shot up, and torched kibbutzes, firing through windows, wresting women and children from safe rooms, trapping others in their burning homes. To cries of "Kill the Jews" in Arabic, they slaughtered, raped, or kidnapped any Israeli they found.

In the end—and after a tragically slow response by Israeli forces—more than 1,200 Israeli citizens were killed, including scores of children. Nearly 7,000 others were injured, and some 240 civilians were taken and dragged back to Gaza as hostages. In Nir Oz, where one-fourth of the kibbutz were either killed or abducted, what remained of a once-thriving community were the burned, crumbling remnants of homes and the horror stories about what happened inside them.

October 7, a Jewish holiday, was the single bloodiest day in the state of Israel since its founding in 1948, and the single deadliest day for Jews since World War II. It was also the day of the largest rocket barrage in Israel's history (more than 2,200 missiles launched from Gaza, some landing as far north as Tel Aviv). It was one of the worst terrorist massacres ever recorded, and its inhuman horrors, many of which were captured on body cameras worn by the invaders, are too horrific, too traumatizing, to even think about. What followed the attack was a furious, unprecedented retaliation by Israeli forces, which stormed Gaza, relentlessly bombed buildings, and killed or injured many tens of thousands of civilians, most of them women and children, while trying to disable Hamas.

It was a dark day that forever changed the world.

I was home in London on October 7, up early, when I checked an alert on my Fox News app and saw the first raw report of missiles being fired from Gaza. I didn't think much of it; we'd get flash reports about shelling in Israel all the time. Then there was the chime of another news alert, and another, and another: more rockets over Israel. At first no one knew the scale of the attack: the full picture would take hours to emerge. Fox News had a team of reporters in Israel, including my friend and fellow foreign correspondent Trey Yingst, and I started reading reports from him about the ceaseless explosion of missiles. Within an hour, Trey arrived in the southern part of Israel that was under siege. His reports made it clear what was happening—the terrorists were pouring in, shooting people, burning homes.

This was a full-scale attack.

That morning in London, as I read about the tragedy playing out in Israel, I felt a familiar urge. It was something I first felt when I was young, and then all through my career as a journalist. As soon as I learned about something big happening somewhere in the world, I wanted to be there. I *needed* to be there. Early on, it was far-flung adventures that called to me, but when I became a correspondent, it was news reports about major world events. It was a little voice inside me saying, *You gotta go, you gotta go, that's your story*. I listened to that voice, and as a journalist I covered basically every major global conflict for fifteen years, often flying out a day or two after hearing about it. Even at Fox News, if someone was assigned to a story I wanted, I would be annoyed. I always wanted to be there, in the middle of the action, experiencing it up close, wherever it was.

Hearing about the terrible events of October 7 was no different.

The little voice went off again, telling me I had to go. The truth is, I was happy to hear the voice. I was glad it was still there. I listened to it, as I always did, but I listened to another voice as well—a voice that said, *Come on, Ben, be reasonable*. It wasn't quite Alicia's voice, but it might as well have been. And, of course, the second voice was right. I understood I couldn't just up and go like I used to. I was no longer physically capable of dodging bullets and bombs.

Even so, I *still* wanted to go. The voice wasn't about to let me off that easy. The Middle East was where I did a lot of my reporting. I knew the area and its history very well. At home in London, I'd been working hard for months on strengthening my body and adapting to my life, but I was starting to get a bit antsy. I needed to do something, go somewhere, tell a big story; I needed it for my mental well-being. I knew Fox usually dispatched as many as three teams to cover big stories—the first team out, then one or two others to do follow-up and human interest stories.

I saw no reason why I couldn't be part of the second or third Fox team.

It was a few days after October 7 that I first mentioned going to Alicia. I suspect she knew it was coming. I'd already traveled to Washington, DC, and Germany, and in a month's time I'd be heading to Ukraine to interview President Zelenskyy. I had proved I was still capable of going places and reporting stories. Even so, I had no desire to immediately ship out to Gaza and report from the front lines. My idea was to wait until things had somewhat settled, then report a story not from Gaza, which was under attack, but from somewhere in Israel.

Before the bombing in Ukraine, I would always soft-pedal the dangers of any assignment when discussing it with Alicia, mainly because I didn't want to worry her unnecessarily, but also because, well, I wanted her to give me her blessing, and I didn't see the point of overdramatizing potential outcomes. Then the bombing changed everything—*except*, I discovered, my tendency to soft-pedal.

When I mentioned Israel to Alicia, I said things like *Perhaps I could go and anchor the coverage, that's all* and *I won't go anywhere near Gaza, where the fighting is* and *I'll be in Tel Aviv, which is sometimes the target of bombs but, you know, they have that incredible air defense system, so I won't be in any real danger.* I didn't want to deceive Alicia, but neither did I want to alarm her. My presentation, I thought, was truthful and reasonable, and I believed I made a solid case for her giving me her blessing.

"Absolutely not," Alicia said when I was finished talking.

I might have argued in the past, but this time I didn't. The events in southern Israel had just happened, and the scale of the horror was shocking beyond belief. The idea of me going anywhere near the Middle East was, in this highly fraught moment, quite obviously not appealing to Alicia. What's more, Alicia has earned all the deference and respect in the world, after what she's gone through. If she said no, then it was no.

At least for the moment.

In the old days, I would have been miserable not going. I remember when Fox asked me to travel to Afghanistan to cover the withdrawal of U.S. troops in August 2021. We had a big family vacation planned, and for one of the only times in my tenure at Fox, I turned down the assignment. A few days into the holiday, a suicide bomber set off a massive explosion at the Abbey Gate of Hamid Karzai International Airport, outside Kabul, killing thirteen U.S. service members and 170 Afghan civilians. Afghanistan became the biggest story in the world. According to Alicia, I moped my way through the rest of the holiday because I hadn't been there to cover this critical story. "You should have just bloody gone," she said.

After the bombing, that desperate nervousness about missing out on a story went away. The urge to cover it didn't, but the frustrated annoyance if I didn't was gone. In London I didn't watch TV coverage of the events in Israel and Gaza and stress about not being there. My life was different now. Yes, I loved my old life, but I loved my new life even more. I defied all the odds by getting back to Alicia and the girls, and being with them was always going to be the most important thing in my life. I had to accept that my life had changed, my career had changed, and I wouldn't be hopping on planes at a moment's notice anymore. I accepted Alicia's judgment, and I went on with all the rituals of my rehab.

But the story didn't go away. Some news stories happen and end in a flash, after a day or two. The Israel-Gaza war did not. It was going to be a long and bloody slog, as the Israel Defense Forces went house to house in Gaza trying to root out Hamas terrorists and find the hidden hostages. I pitched Fox News on a series of shows from Israel that focused on survivors and hostages who'd been returned. I wouldn't be the guy on the front line doing live hits; I'd be off on my own digging deeper into personal stories. My colleague and boss, Jay Wallace, the president of Fox News Media—someone who threw the full force of the network behind getting me safely out of Ukraine—was typically supportive.

"Go ahead," he said. "Do it."

About three months after the October 7 attack, I sat down with Alicia again and talked about taking the trip.

This time the conversation lasted a bit longer. We discussed all the details, all the pros and cons of going, and in the end Alicia gave me her blessing—as long as I promised to stay away from Gaza, where the war raged on.

Alicia understands what drives me and why I need to continue with my career. Since the bombing, she has asked me to be more measured and patient and not leap blindly into assignments, but she has yet to ever stop me from going somewhere I really wanted to go. Even now, with me limping around in my prosthetics, she wasn't going to say no.

Within a few weeks of Alicia signing off, I packed my bags and, in early 2024, boarded a plane headed to Tel Aviv.

*   *   *

When I arrived, I connected with Yael Rotem Kuriel, a veteran Fox News producer based in Jerusalem. Talking to Yael made it clear that, to the journalists who lived and worked in Israel, this was no ordinary story. It was personal. Everyone knew someone who knew someone who had been at the Supernova Sukkot Gathering, the open-air music festival in the western Negev desert, about three miles from the Gaza border, where Hamas terrorists armed with AK-47s swooped in from the sky on motorized hang gliders (more arrived via trucks and motorbikes) and massacred 364 civilian concertgoers. Everyone knew or knew of one of the forty or so civilians who had been dragged from the festival and held hostage. It was clear that Yael and everyone else at the bureau were deeply, emotionally involved in this story. In a way, they were even *part* of the story. It fell to them to bear witness to what happened, and to tell the world about it.

One of the stories I felt I had to tell was that of the hostages. The fact that these souls were violently wrested from their families and unable to get back home to them hit a particular nerve with me. In late November 2023, Hamas released 105 Israeli hostages in exchange for around 180 Palestinian prisoners and a weeklong cease-fire in Gaza. The returning hostages would need varying amounts of medical attention and physical rehabilitation, but none of them would escape months and months of mental recovery. Their families in Israeli kept a tight arm around them, shielding them from the media so they could adjust to being back home in peace. As a result, booking an interview with one of the freed hostages was tricky.

While Yael and I worked on that, we also decided to visit one of the damaged kibbutzes in southern Israel and speak to survivors there. We settled on the Nir Oz Kibbutz, which sat on roughly twenty-seven acres in the northwestern Negev desert. Founded in 1955, it had only seventy residents and four trees in its early days, but over the decades Nir Oz became a model of low-water landscaping, using desalinated and recycled water to raise lush, vast, flourishing gardens and even grow asparagus for export. Four hundred Israelis lived there in single-story homes, in a kind of communal utopian splendor, with turkeys and peacocks roaming the grasses and children laughing on seesaws.

Yet no kibbutz suffered more death and damage on October 7 than Nir Oz, and Yael and I and our team decided to focus our attention there. We traveled by armored van to the remnants of the kibbutz and set up interviews with some of the survivors, who lived in temporary housing and returned to the kibbutz to speak with us.

What we saw when we got there was shocking.

There were few signs of life in Nir Oz, but many of destruction. The homes that remained weren't homes anymore: they were charred walls and collapsed roofs pocked with bullet holes. The streets were littered with rubble and torched debris—tricycles, strollers, a blackened saxophone, the shells of burned-out cars. Most of the lush vegetation remained, including lovely rosemary bushes and a regal ficus tree, but that only served to highlight the utter devastation around them. Inside the shells of homes there were ruined chairs and sofas and burned walls and safe-room doors that had been pried open by terrorists who spent hours hunting every last citizen of Nir Oz. The massacre had happened weeks earlier, but the kibbutz still somehow held every agony, ever inhuman crime visited on it on October 7.

Some surviving members of the kibbutz walked Yael and I through these horrible ruins. It was a slow, somber walk. The survivors were heavy-hearted and, in some cases, apparently still in shock. Yet they were determined to tell their stories in full. They felt the world needed to know about the atrocity that happened on their little patch of earth.

"With friends from the kibbutz it is something else, because you know them your entire life and you know their families and you spend all day together," Lotus Lahav, a twenty-two-year-old survivor of the attack, told me. "You wake up and have breakfast together, then you go to the pool together, then you go to the pub together in the evening."

In the idyllic days before the attack, the only outward sign that Nir Oz wasn't a pure paradise was the chain-link fence topped with coiled barbed wire around its perimeter. One of the communities closest to Gaza, Nir Oz had seen missile attacks from Hamas before, and every house was equipped with a *mamad*, Hebrew for safe room. Still, the threat of harm seemed remote enough for many to forgo functional locks on their safe-room doors. "You'd hear the siren and jump out of bed and run to the safe room, and then you'd hear the explosion and wait a few seconds and come out and get back to normal," Lotus explained.

That all changed on October 7.

I sat with Lotus and her mother, Irit Lahav, as they described the attack they endured together in their home. That morning they heard the sirens and ran barefoot in their pajamas to the safe room. Soon they heard gunfire close by, and in the early morning darkness they saw young men with guns through their windows. They logged on to the WhatsApp community chat and learned they were under attack.

> Two terrorists on a motorcycle by the bypass road.
> Shooting in our neighborhood.
> Stay in safe rooms and lock doors.

But the door to the Lahavs' safe room didn't lock. In the dark and shaking with fear, Irit and Lotus fashioned a crossbar to fortify the door, using an aluminum Dyson vacuum cleaner tube and a thick wooden stick lashed together with a leather cord. They also built a wall out of hard-backed books and crouched behind it under a table, hoping, as Irit put it, to only be injured, not killed. Seven or eight terrorists burst in shouting and shooting and spent hours trying to pry open or fire through the safe-room door to get to the Lahavs.

"I knew," Lotus told me, "that these were the last few seconds of my life."

On the WhatsApp group chat the horror kept unfolding.

> The Giberman family need help! A terrorist in their house!
> House is on fire and I'm suffocating.
> We are burning.

One by one, participants disappeared from the group chat as the massacre ran up its deadly toll.

Huddled together under the table, terrorists pounding and firing at the door and shouting *Allahu akbar*, Irit and Lotus quietly said their goodbyes. "I told her I am so grateful for the twenty-two years we spent together," said Irit. Lotus said, "I had a very good life. I had fun. Now, it's time."

*   *   *

Somehow, the makeshift crossbar held.

In my time with Irit and Lotus, I was struck by how composed and articulate they were, and by how they described what happened in an even, measured way. But I also sensed that, just beneath the surface, all the pain and fear and dread and panic and disillusionment were still there, and likely indelible. They had confronted the very worst of human nature, and fought for their lives, and lost and suffered so much, and it was clear they would never be the same—that October 7 had changed them forever.

But they were there, still alive, holding their ground. Their defiance was miraculous and powerful, and that, I understood, was the real story I had come to find. It was their uncommon *resilience*, in the face of unspeakable adversity, that drew me to Israel to help them share their sorrow and strength.

Another survivor I spoke with in Nir Oz was just as strong in her resolve—and just as devastated by the nightmare of October 7. Amit Siman Tov, forty years old, barricaded herself and her family in their safe room and survived three separate assaults on the door in the span of eight hours. When the terrorists set their house on fire and smoke poured into the room, the family—Amit, her husband, and their children, ages nine, six, and two—shoved urine-soaked rags against the foot of the door and took turns breathing through a small crack in the window. "My daughter was pleading with me, 'Mom, open the door, let them shoot me, I don't want to be burned to death,'" Amit recalled through tears. "This sentence that came out of her . . . it froze my soul."

The family made it through the horror, but six other members of Amit's family did not, including her brother, his wife, and their three young children, who all perished.

"My brother, he was writing with us, texting with us until around nine fifteen," Amit told me. "Then at quarter to ten his wife wrote in a mothers' group chat, 'We've been shot,' and a minute after that she wrote, 'I am seriously injured.' And that was it." Knowing that her brother's family was under attack but not being able to help them is one of many unbearable thoughts Amit struggles to get out of her head.

"I can't even explain what I felt like," she said. "Fifty meters away, someone is killing your family, and there is nothing you can do because someone is trying to kill you too."

Amit allowed me to tour the remains of her brother's torched home with her. The experience was overwhelming. Amit had been there before, but not without a facial mask to block her view of the charred walls and shattered household items. She showed me the safe-room door, which was riddled with bullet holes but did not give in. But while the terrorists never made it inside, some of their bullets got through, and Amit's brother and his wife died of gunshot wounds. Their three children—who were roughly the same ages as my three daughters—later burned alive in that room. Thoughts about the children's final moments, Amit said, "are the very worst thoughts I have."

The trip to Nir Oz and my conversations with several survivors were heavier and more intense than I could have imagined. Yes, I was in awe of how poised and resolute all the survivors were, and how they believed that speaking of what happened to them was their sacred duty. But at the same time, it was impossible to escape the terrible, palpable gloom that hung over the remnants of the kibbutz and all the people who had so happily lived there. The community, once brimming with life and dreams, was now a solemn, desolate ghost town, stripped of nearly all that mattered. The terrorists, who wore maps of the kibbutz on their vests directing them to places like the kindergarten school, made sure of that. "Everything that we had was taken from us," Irit Lahav told me. "Everything. Our houses, our neighbors, our families."

Or as another survivor I spoke with, Ola Metzger, told me, "I really don't want to say that we are totally broken, I really don't. But—only time will tell."

As true as that may have been, the ultimate takeaway for me was still the uncommon resilience of the survivors. Their unshakable faith—in God, in family, in each other—sustained them and kept them from falling apart. That was the real story of what happened at Nir Oz. And it's why it was easy to come up with a title for my report. I simply used the English translation of the Hebrew words *Nir Oz*:

Meadow of Strength.

* * *

While we were at the kibbutz, Yael and I kept hustling to secure an interview with one of the released hostages. It wasn't going well. The net of security around them was tight, and sometimes asking for an interview felt like we were callously willing to invade their privacy at the expense of their mental health. Yael and I were careful in our approaches, but we were also getting a bit desperate. Several days had passed and we still hadn't lined up an interview, and I believed the only way I could convey the scale and breadth of what happened on October 7 and beyond was by speaking to someone who'd been held in Gaza.

I spoke with as many people as I could, looking for anyone who could put me in touch with one of the freed hostages, to no avail. We did secure an interview with a psychologist who counseled several of the hostages, and that was helpful. At the end of the interview, I went up to the psychologist and pleaded my case.

"Look, we really want to convey what happened to the world, and we really need to speak with someone who was there," I pleaded. "Is there any chance you could connect me to one of the hostages so I could speak with them?"

To my surprise, the psychologist immediately said, "Yes, I think there is."

At the wire, with only a couple of days to go, we had our interview. I would be speaking with Maya Regev, an extraordinary young woman who was kidnapped from the Supernova festival and held hostage in Gaza for fifty days. It so happened that Maya had injuries that were similar to the ones I sustained in Ukraine—her legs were riddled by bullets and her left foot had nearly been severed from her leg. Even before I met her, I felt a kinship with her. I understood the nature of the challenge she faced.

We set up for an interview in her room at the Sheba Medical Center in Tel Aviv. Normally I would enter at the same time as my camera-man, and the subject and I would talk while the camera was being set up, a process that sometimes took thirty minutes. This time I asked the crew to set up the camera first, before I entered, so I wouldn't have to bother Maya with mundane chitchat. Considering what she'd been through, I didn't want to be more disruptive than necessary.

In her room, Maya—twenty-one at the time of her abduction—sat in a wheelchair with one leg bandaged and the other propped up and held in place by round metal rods. I sat in a chair opposite her. Maya's father, Ilan Regev, stayed in the room, watching over her. There was a heaviness in the room, and a sense of mourning, and I understood why—Maya's dear friend Omer, who attended the music festival with her, remained a hostage in Gaza.

Maya herself was strong and steady. Slight in stature but towering in demeanor, she held her jaw tight and bravely dove into the story of October 7. Once she started speaking, she barely stopped for an hour, and I only had to ask a handful of questions. She made it clear that she needed to tell her story because Omer was still in Gaza. She needed the world to know what happened, and what was still happening.

When I asked her about the day of the Supernova music festival, which she attended with Omer and her younger brother Itay, eighteen, a slight smile appeared. "We were very excited about it," she said. "Like [for] two months, before everyone was talking about it. It was a big event and everyone wanted to go." At the festival Maya danced with Omer and Itay; in footage from the event, she is utterly carefree and happy. But at 6:29 a.m., "they shut the music down and told us that there are rockets," Maya said. "And at first we didn't understand."

Within seconds, Maya heard gunshots and explosions, and saw men armed with rifles dropping down from the sky. "Everyone is running hysterically," she told me. "Everyone, like tons of people. And everywhere we went, we heard gunshots. In every direction, we heard gunshots. And that way we were surrounded, like we had no chance."

The trio made it to their parked car but soon found themselves behind a truckload of Hamas terrorists. Eight or nine men jumped off and shot directly at Maya's car. "Like, spraying the car," Maya said. "Tons of bullets." Some of those bullets tore into Maya's legs and shattered the bones. Her left foot was so badly shot that it dangled from the bottom of her leg, nearly detached. Maya felt the pain, she said, "but I was more scared than in pain. So I didn't let it control me."

The terrorists tied up Itay and Omer and threw them into the back of a pickup truck. Maya was bound and put between two Hamas militants, one of whom tortured her as they drove away. "I told him 'please stop, I'm in pain,'" Maya recalled. "But he just looked at me, laughed and continued."

The terrorists paraded their captives through the streets of Gaza. Maya refused to look up and let the cheering crowds see her face, but one of the terrorists grabbed her hair and forced her up. They soon arrived at an entrance to one of Gaza's notorious underground tunnels, where Maya was made to hobble through the dark and narrow passageways on her nearly severed foot. The floor was littered with rocks and the hostages were forced to walk in their socks, and Maya felt agonizing pain. But she continued jumping forward on one leg riddled with bullets, fearful that if she stopped, she would die.

After a while, Maya was taken to the home of a Palestinian family, where she was kept for the next five days. She shared a bed with an Arab woman who rationalized the violence of October 7. Maya's injuries were so severe that her abductors dressed her up in Arabic garments and snuck her into a Gazan hospital. There her dangling foot was reattached incorrectly, at an angle. She also had surgery to remove the bullets that had been inside her for eight days.

One day, a Palestinian doctor entered her room and asked Maya her name. She stuck to the story and gave her fake Arabic name, but the doctor recognized her from media stories about her abduction. "And he starts screaming at me and he grabbed me by my foot and just lifted my leg and started swinging it really hard while he's screaming at me and telling me I'm a murderer and my people are murderers and we kill everybody and we are wrong and I deserve everything," Maya stoically told me. "And I'm just crying, telling him to stop and trying to tell him I'm also a victim of this war."

By then the Israeli siege of Gaza had begun, and one Israeli bomb landed close enough to the hospital to shatter the windows in Maya's room and shake her bed. "I thought about my family a lot," Maya said—thoughts that kept her strong throughout her ordeal. But she also thought of the phone call she made to her father, Ilan, during the festival attack—a call in which she screamed and cried and sounded desperately panicked, and a call she knew must have left her father heartbroken and disconsolate. "She called me at eight forty-seven a.m.," Ilan told me in a separate interview later that day. "She shout, 'Bad men come, they killing me, I'm going to die.'"

In my career, I had listened to many, many stories of unthinkable harm and torture inflicted on the innocent. I'd sat across from many victims of such horrors and watched them bravely work their way through their stories with remarkable strength and clarity. I'd developed enough hard skin, as journalists must do, to make it through these interviews with a kind of professional detachment. But that wasn't possible with Maya. Maybe it was because she had, like me, a severely damaged leg, and she sat with it propped up and heavily bandaged, just as I had with mine for many months during my recovery. I felt a special kinship with Maya, and for a moment I forgot I was a journalist interviewing her for a TV report. It felt more like I was visiting a friend and listening as she shared her terrible experience. I found Maya's strength uniquely inspiring and moving.

After a month in captivity, Maya heard rumblings about a possible release of hostages in a prisoner exchange. She didn't get her hopes up; she wasn't a child or elderly or a mother, and she didn't think she'd be among the first hostages released. Then she heard that she could indeed be among the first twenty-four hostages sent back to Israel, because her injuries needed urgent medical care. After fifty long days as a hostage, Maya was driven through a checkpoint in Rafa, on the Egyptian border, before being taken to a Red Cross facility in Israel. She was free. "But even in the car, I was always scared that maybe someone is going to shoot at the car and I'm going to die," Maya told me. "I thought, *I'm not safe yet.*"

It was only when two female Israeli soldiers and an Israeli doctor came into the ambulance with her that Maya finally believed she was safe and free. "The moment they closed the ambulance door, I started crying like I couldn't believe it," Maya said. "I thought, *This is really happening.*"

Still, Maya did not feel true relief until her brother Itay was released four days later. Even then, when it was clear that Omer would not be coming home, Maya could not bring herself to celebrate her freedom and reunion with her family. "It was bittersweet, because Omer and so many others are still being held in Gaza," she explained. "I'm very sad about Omer. That's why I try to do whatever I can do."

Maya's recovery will be long and arduous. She had surgery to properly align her left foot and received antibiotics for months to treat her many infections. She had constant physiotherapy, visits from doctors, batteries of tests—a routine I understood well. But Maya, I instantly knew, had the fortitude and resolve she would need to make it back from her injuries and, as is her hope, dance and run one day. "All I think about is being healed and to walk again," she said.

The message she wanted to convey to the world was one of defiance and hope. "Tell the world about what really is happening," she said to me. "I'm really trying to do that right now because I still have friends there that I really care about and I know how hard it is to be there. So, I keep fighting for them because they can't talk, they can't scream what they want to scream, and so I scream for them here."

The interview was remarkable. I was floored by Maya's steady and purposeful presence, by her intelligence, by her determination to use her freedom to help those still in captivity. She has been a shining example of the power of the human spirit, and I felt honored to help her share her story. But there was something else about her that stayed with me, because of my own ordeal in Ukraine. Maya told me that, even when a band of terrorists leaped from a truck and sprayed her car with bullets, she did not, for a moment, believe she wouldn't make it.

"I always knew that I would go home," she said. "I didn't know how long it would take, but I always knew I will see my family again. I remember looking at the floor of the car when they were shooting and telling myself, 'No, this is not the end of you. You are not going to die. I have so many things that I need to do in my life, there's no way I'm going to die here. So, it's okay.'"

I understood Maya's words. That was exactly how I felt when I was lying on the ground after the bombing, seemingly doomed but nevertheless certain I'd make it home. Not for an instant did I doubt that I would see Alicia and our daughters again, or that I would be with them soon, holding them and assuring them I was okay. It was not wishful thinking. It was not false bravado. It was something inside me that was unbreakable, that could not be moved or diminished. It was the *core* of me.

*   *   *

The time I spent with the survivors of Nir Oz and with Maya Regev was deeply affecting, and each one of them was profoundly strong and resilient. The interviews I recorded were, I believed, powerful and profound, and I couldn't wait to get back home and put my reports together. Yet as successful as the trip had been in journalistic terms, the nature and details of the tragedy Yael and I covered would stay with us for a long, long time. It was a singularly emotional story for Yael to cover, yet she and the rest of the Fox News crew never wavered from their professional obligation to report on the incident fully and fairly. Like me, they were able to push aside their emotions long enough to impartially get the story. But that didn't mean those emotions went away. Shortly after we'd wrapped up the assignment, Yael, who'd been tireless and stalwart in making it all possible, finally let down her guard.

"After this," she told me, "I think I have to take a step back, take a few days off. It was all just so intense."

What happened on October 7 happened, in a way, to every Israeli everywhere, and especially to those who lived there. Yael knew people who had been killed or abducted, and her need to tell the world what happened was deeply personal. Standing in Nir Oz, in the wake of so much death and destruction, acutely affected her, as it did me. This was not a story you could just shake off and walk away from. At Fox News, we have continued to report on the turmoil in Israel, as well as on the thousands of innocent victims of the bombings in Gaza. After working on the story, I signed up to be part of a program that helps send prosthetics to the injured in Gaza who, like me, need to be put back together.

My time in Israel pushed me to once again contemplate my mortality. When I thought back on the bombing in Ukraine, I rarely wondered why I had survived when the four others in my car did not. But I *did* occasionally ask that question. *Why me? Was God looking out for me? Or was it random chance? Why was I saved when others weren't?* In time, I came to believe these were not the right questions to be asking. The right question was:

What will I do with this gift I've been given?

I've said that the real story of October 7 is about resilience. But it is also about another powerful force: faith. Faith is a product of contemplation, in that it springs from deep, reflective thought. Faith is forged when we look inside and search for the core of who we are. What is it that sustains us? That empowers us? What is the ground we can build our lives on? For those in Nir Oz and other communities in Israel, the sustaining, empowering force was faith—faith in Judaism, faith in their communities, faith in the ultimate triumph of good over evil. Faith is what makes them resilient.

This kind of contemplation of our innermost identity—our core selves—is, I've come to think, a crucial part of overcoming challenges and recovering from setbacks. Since the bombing, I've spent a lot of time thinking about what matters most to me, what gives me strength, what it is that I place my faith in. Some will answer that question by saying God and religion, and certainly, having been raised a Christian, I believe in God and draw strength from Him. Others will say their faith rests in something or someone else. For me, contemplation always brings me back to the same place, the same four people:

Alicia and the girls.

I remember the night I returned to London from Israel, and how happy and relieved I was to be able to see and hug Alicia again. That night, in a quiet moment after the girls went to bed, we talked about how the trip had been different from all my other assignments as a journalist.

"For the first time," I told Alicia, "I think I understood what these people I interviewed were actually going through."

I had always believed that as a journalist I had to remain disconnected from the subjects of my interviews. I didn't think I should try to feel what they were feeling. Empathizing with victims and their plight was not really part of my job. But in Israel, I found that this empathy came naturally. It was impossible for me *not* to feel what these people were feeling, because I'd gone through a similar experience and understood the kinds of challenges they were facing. Their words and sentiments made more sense to me; they gave me a new way into these stories, through emotions and not just facts.

What really surprised me, though, was that I instantly understood that this new dynamic between me and Maya and the other survivors actually made me a *better* journalist. It allowed me to dig deeper into their stories, to ask more pointed questions, to more closely follow the threads of their internal struggles. Talking to Alicia about all this was a *huge* moment for me not only as a journalist but also as a human being. Alicia helped me see that becoming more empathetic was one of the hidden blessings of the bombing, and a milestone in my life and career.

That night, Alicia and I talked some more about the Israel trip but also about the deeper implications of the event that changed both our lives—the bombing in Ukraine.

Alicia wondered if being a father and having young children was part of the reason why I found the strength to make it out of Ukraine and back to my family. Having her and the girls to come back to, she said, may have been the difference. That I wanted to get back to them *so badly* may have given me something extra and undefined that propelled me forward. I found it hard to argue with that. After all, it was my beautiful daughters, Iris, Honor, and Hero, who called out to me when I lay unconscious in the burning car, seconds away from oblivion. It was they who empowered me to rise out of the blackness of my imminent death and somehow get out of the car. My core, as I've said before, is my family. I put my faith in them.

When I was in Nir Oz, I was technically bending the promise I made to Alicia that I wouldn't go anywhere near the fighting in Gaza.

My father, Roderick Hall, a U.S. Army private with the Seventh Infantry, at the Thirty-Eighth Parallel, the former border between North and South Korea. He served there near the end of the Korean War.

My mother, Jenny, and I in Spain in 1987. Her sense of adventure and eagerness to talk to anyone shaped my life and career.

Yes, that's me at age eleven, playing the lead role of Amahl in the popular opera *Amahl and the Night Visitors* on a tour in Nashville. My character learns to walk again—strangely prophetic.

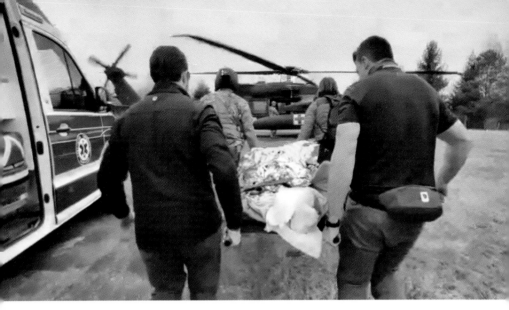

Only when U.S. military personnel loaded me into a Blackhawk helicopter in eastern Poland did I finally allow myself to think I was safe.

(COURTESY OF SAVE OUR ALLIES)

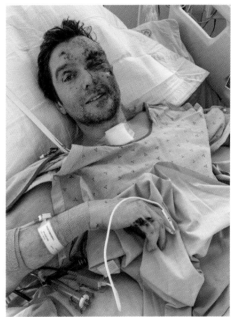

This is only three days after the bombing, when I was pretty banged up and just beginning my recovery in Landstuhl, Germany.

One of my hardest days was aboard the cavernous C-17 military cargo plane that flew me from Germany to Texas in 2022. It was a painful twenty-four-hour journey.

This is the moment at BAMC when John Ferguson and Del Lipe slipped a silicone lining on my right knee and measured me for my first prosthetic limb.

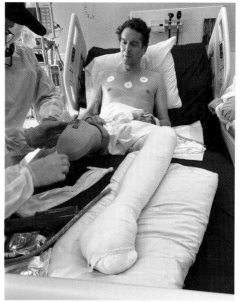

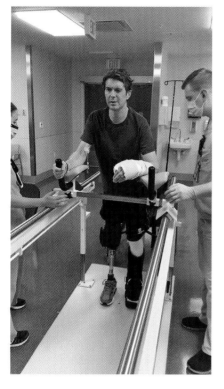

And this is the first step I took with a crude early version of my prosthetic leg. It might not look it, but this tiny step was monumental for me.

This is me with the people who saved my life—the amazing staff at Brooke Army Medical Center's ICU Burn Unit. I returned to thank them all in November 2023, about twenty months after the bombing.

As a journalist I tried hard to never make myself the story, yet after the bombing, that's what I became. My wife, Alicia, and our daughters, Hero, Iris, and Honor, helped me celebrate my first book in 2023.

Me hanging out with my kids and the three daughters of my wonderful friend, Sarah Verardo. Children were usually far less intimidated to approach and ask about my legs than anyone.

Some of the beautiful cards and letters of support I received while recovering, from across the U.S. and the world. I continue to write back to everyone and thank them with all my heart.

I believe firmly in pushing yourself to try new things and learn new things. Here I am changing a smoke alarm at home, on prosthetic legs I'm still learning to use. I remember Alicia anxiously asked, "Are you sure this is a good idea?" Absolutely!

Shiver me timbers! Here I am, having fun on Halloween with Iris and Hero. I chose the pirate get-up as a way to embrace the new me—pretty convincing, I think!

Planting a young olive tree in front of the London home Alicia and I bought together after we were married. We watched it grow alongside our family and were sad to leave it.

Hero, Iris, Honor, and I on a family vacation to Portugal in 2024 (Alicia took the photo). Walking on sand with prosthetics was tricky, but, as with everything else, I got the hang of it.

If there's any possible way I can join my girls in an adventure, I'm going to find it and join in. Here we are frog hunting in Portugal.

We spend the holidays in Alicia's native Australia when we can. Here we are in Sydney with Santa Claus who, because Christmas comes in summer in Australia, sometimes wears boardshorts.

The girls joined me in my home studio in London and took turns anchoring the news desk. I resumed reporting for Fox just a few months after returning to London after the bombing.

Back at the Fox News Bureau in New York City after my recovery. Fox and everyone there have been heroic in their ceaseless efforts to not only save my life but get me back to work.

Returning to journalism was one of the goals that helped me get through my long initial recovery. In 2024, I anchored Fox News Sunday in the DC Bureau for the first time.

(FOX NEWS)

It was pretty painful learning to monoski at a London ski club in 2023. But you must never let that stop you.

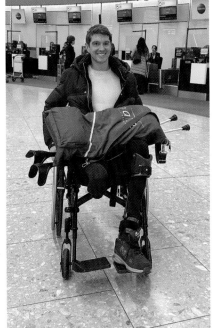

My first overseas trip after my recovery was to the Correspondent's Dinner in Washington, DC. I'd injured myself and had to use a wheelchair, and hit a few rough spots, but again, never let that stop you.

Here I am behind the scenes at the Correspondent's Dinner in 2023. My great friend and agent Olivia Metzger is to my right and, just above her, Fox News anchor Martha MacCallum.

At the dinner with (*from left*) Dr. Rich Jadick, Sarah Verardo, Bo, Fox News's exceptional Jennifer Griffin, and General Charles Q. Brown Jr., the chairman of the Joint Chiefs of Staff.

U.S. Secretary of State Antony Blinken welcoming me back to the State Department in 2024. My return to Washington, where I'd anchored from before the bombing, had been another huge goal for me.

(COURTESY OF STATE DEPT)

6/2023

My interview with Blinken was anything but ceremonial, and I took the chance to push him on Ukraine and foreign policy, as the secretary kindly noted in his inscription.

Ben - So good to see you back in action, even on the Receiving end of your typically tough (but fair) questions. With admiration, Antony Blinken

I was privileged to be able to cover the Invictus Games in Dusseldorf in 2023—but I was also honored to be asked to present medals to the three inspirational finalists in the archery competition.

At the Invictus Games I interviewed several athletes and asked what the Games meant to them. They all said training and competing gave them purpose and made them feel alive—something I understood.

After the bombing I knew I'd someday return to Ukraine, and in 2023 I finally did. Here I am heading to Kiev on the same train line my rescuers used to spirit me out of the country, saving my life. I spent the time reliving the journey out.

Perhaps my proudest moment was simply walking off the train in Kyiv under my own power. By contrast (*below*), I had to be carried off the train that took me to safety a few days after the bombing.

(FOX NEWS)

Three days after the bombing, I had to be carried off the train at the Polish-Ukraine border following a ten-hour, pretty brutal ride to safety.

(COURTESY OF SAVE OUR ALLIES)

My trip to Ukraine was at the invitation of President Volodymyr Zelenskyy, who presented me the Order of Merit, III Class, for supporting "Ukraine's independence and territorial integrity."

In Kyiv, I got to thank the Ukrainian doctors and nurses who stitched me up after the bombing. The man in the green shirt is Dr. Volodymyr Grygorovskyy, the surgeon who kept me alive.

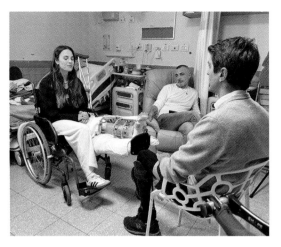

This is me with Maya Regev (and her father, Ilan) in a Tel Aviv hospital in 2024. Maya spent fifty-one days as a Hamas hostage in Gaza before being released. Her courage and resolve are extraordinary.

(FOX NEWS)

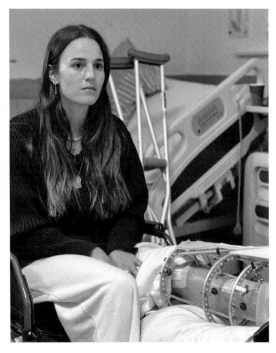

Like me, Maya suffered gruesome leg injuries that left her with a long, difficult rehab process. "All I think about," she told me in our interview, "is being healed and to walk again."

(FOX NEWS)

On my trip to Israel I reported from the ruins of the Nir Oz kibbutz, nearly destroyed by Hamas terrorists on Oct. 7, 2023. The survivors I spoke with were strong and steadfast but often still in shock.

(FOX NEWS)

In my search for stories about resilience, I found the remarkable folks in Hazard, Kentucky, who rebuilt their dying town. Here I am on Main Street with the Fox crew, my arm around Hazard Mayor "Happy" Mobelini.

I interviewed several citizens of Hazard about their struggles and the rebirth of the town. As one of them said of the turnaround, "It was David versus Goliath, and no one thought we could win but us."

In 2023 I spoke to eight hundred American military nurses at Royal Air Force Lakenheath in Suffolk, England. "Whenever I really needed it," I told them, "I always had a nurse there to tell me, 'I got your back.'"

In May 2024 I gave the commencement speech at the Institute of World Politics in DC. My message to graduates: whatever hardship you might end up facing, you have what it takes to overcome it.

(COURTESY OF INSTITUTE OF WORLD POLITICS)

I got in a little rooftop putting over Sixth Avenue during a photo shoot for *Golf Digest*. After the bombing I resumed golfing and amazingly got better, I even beat my father-in-law in a friendly match.

(FOX NEWS)

I may never make it to Broadway but I did make it to Times Square. Here, a billboard touts my Fox News podcast, *Searching for Heroes*.

Without Alicia, I wouldn't have anywhere near the blessed life I have today. She is my rock, my person, and my best friend—she gives me all my strength.

At my very lowest moments after the bombing—including in the seconds after it happened—I thought about my beautiful family. I hope that since then I've become a better man, husband, and father.

(COURTESY OF RICK FINDLER)

Our little crew (*clockwise from left*): Hero, Iris, Honor, and baby Sage. I know for certain that together, as a family, there is no obstacle we can't overcome.

I told her I'd mainly be in Tel Aviv, and that maybe we'd slip out to interview some survivors of the attacks. But I didn't tell her that we'd slip a full seventy miles south and end up less than two miles from the Gaza border. I felt guilty about not telling her, and even though I felt completely safe in Nir Oz, I vowed to tell Alicia where I'd been just as soon as the assignment was over.

I never got the chance. One day when I was down by the border, I got a text message on my cell phone. I opened it and saw a little map that identified my precise location, represented by a little mark that seemed to sit on the border itself. The text was from Alicia. I'd left the tracker open on my cell, and when Alicia checked my location, I was busted.

Kinda close to Gaza, aren't you? she texted.

When we spoke a bit later, I assured Alicia that I was perfectly safe in Nir Oz. Alicia told me that was exactly what I said about being in Kyiv. Of course, she was right. I tended to minimize danger, and I should have been more honest.

But here's the thing: Alicia understood why I was there, by the border. She knew what had driven me to go. Yes, my life was different now. It would never be the same as it was again. Nor would I ever prioritize anything over Alicia and the girls; they would always be the bottom line. But that didn't mean I had to live in a world where I was afraid to do things. And doing things always carries some risk.

When I made it back home to London, I felt many things. I felt satisfaction that the assignment had gone well. I felt inspired to see how the human spirit can be so badly bruised and battered and nearly broken, but never defeated. I mourned the loss of so many beautiful souls in Israel, as well as all the innocent people who have died in Gaza, and I felt heartbroken for all the families whose loved ones perished. I felt a kinship with Maya Regev, and with other survivors who showed such incredible resolve.

Most of all, I felt blessed. Blessed by Alicia and Iris and Hero and Honor—my family. They are and always will be my core, my faith. In such a dangerous and troubled world, having them is the blessing I cherish most.

12

THE BIGGER THING

Fall 2022

BROOKE ARMY MEDICAL CENTER

Fort Sam Houston, Texas

I passed it by a dozen times and never went in. But it was always there, always open, waiting for when I was ready.

It was a small room on the ground floor of the Brooke Army Medical Center, the hospital where I was recovering from the bombing. Straight across from it was the cafeteria, which I called the canteen, and a mail station where patients picked up packages from home. Like the canteen and the mail station, this room was a practical, purposeful amenity for wounded patients, a place to go and *get* something valuable and needed. Still, I didn't go.

"Not today," I'd say. "Not ready for that yet."

I'd been more or less confined to my room since arriving at BAMC ten days after the bombing in March 2022. Those early weeks of recovery were brutal and painful, with surgeries and procedures every week and tests and needles every day. Not that there was anywhere I could have gone—I'd lost my right leg and most of my left foot, and my prosthetic limbs were still weeks away. The best I could do was climb in a wheelchair and get pushed around the floor. Finally, the doctors let me take my first trip out of the ward. My great friend Jock, who'd been with me in Ukraine and stayed with me while I was at BAMC, got behind my wheelchair and steered me out of my room and to the lobby.

It was like being reborn. It was the first time I felt even a semblance of freedom in a long while, and just wheeling through the ground-floor hallway, away from the MRI or X-ray machines, was exhilarating. Jock took us to the canteen, but before we could go in a woman dashed out of the mail station and ran over to me. She worked at the station and her name was Anichka, and she was from Ukraine. She knew what happened to me and she'd heard I was at BAMC. When she saw me, she burst into tears.

"Benjamin Hall!" she said, wrapping me in a big hug. "What you've done for our country, we can never thank you enough. We're thinking of you and we're here with you and whatever you need, let me know."

I got a bit teary-eyed myself. I believed I knew what I represented to Anichka—the strength and resilience of her fellow Ukrainians, who were so proudly, defiantly refusing to buckle under Putin's assault. So many good citizens and soldiers hadn't made it, *but I was the one who was here.* The survivor, broken but unbowed. My recovery was her recovery too, and I found that deeply moving. More than anything, though, at that moment, I thought about my friend and Fox News cameraman Pierre Zakrzewski, and about Sasha, our fixer, who were both killed by the bombing I survived, a loss I will never get over. For me, Pierre was the one who *wasn't* here, and I missed him terribly.

Just then, I looked to my right. There it was, just a few feet away—the room I'd been avoiding. Two richly polished wood doors with stained-glass panels under six large, raised chrome letters: CHAPEL.

Not today, I thought.

*   *   *

God and religion have been part of my life for as long as I can remember. My father was a strict Catholic and raised me to be one too. My mother supported our upbringing in Catholicism, but she would always say her true religion was nature—walking in the woods, sitting under a tree, feeling part of something bigger than herself. She found God in the hills and fields and moors. Out of this combination of practices and beliefs I shaped my own relationship with God, which has changed throughout my life and been deep and devout at times and, at others, questioning.

For my first Holy Communion my father gave me a Bible, and I remember sitting down with it and reading it front to back in one year. It was bound in beautiful dark leather and I liked how it felt to hold, and as for the story inside, I couldn't get enough of it. What an adventure it was! The gritty, vibrant world it created was unlike anything I'd experienced before, and every time I opened the Bible it felt like an invitation to escape to this faraway place of drama and intrigue and miracles and holiness. I loved every minute of reading it, and I still have that Bible somewhere, waiting for me to dip back into it. More than anything, it made me feel, just as my mother had, like I was part of something much bigger than myself.

When I was a teenager my parents decided we would spend several months in rural France, living in a convent while we worked on a house nearby. The sounds of chanting nuns filled our days. Here was more exposure to the strict rituals and trappings of devotion. When construction on our house was finally finished and we moved in, we invited the housemaster of my boarding school, Father Jeremy, to come stay with us. Father Jeremy brought along some holy water and holy wine to bless the house.

Then, a crisis. Father Jeremy kept the holy wine in an ordinary plastic Evian bottle, and one day my mother tossed it in the rubbish, not realizing what it was. When Father Jeremy, moments before the ceremony, asked if anyone had seen his bottle, my mother's face sank to the floor. I can remember her pleading cry: "*I didn't know it was holy!*" Panic ensued, and my mother drove my brother and me to the local dump, where we dove into a huge pile of trash and searched frantically for the missing holy wine. In retrospect I can appreciate the humor of that scene, but at the time it could not have been more serious. After a half hour of urgent digging, we finally found the bottle, and all was right with the world again.

Another time, my brother and I took part in a benediction staged by our neighboring nuns. We carried candles as the nuns sang majestic Gregorian chants in a small chapel in the convent. At one point my brother lowered his head a bit too close to the candle and caught his overly gelled hair on fire. I looked over and saw the top of his head burst into flame. All of us acolytes ran over and whacked away at my brother's head, trying to put out the fire, but not for a second did the nuns stop chanting. And when we finally tamped out the last flicker, we took our seats and resumed chanting as if nothing at all had happened.

In France we also had a donkey named Zaza, who lived with the horses on our property. Every Christmas, Zaza was loaned out to play Mary's donkey in the manger scene in the midnight mass. The smallest infant in the village played the swaddled baby Jesus lying on his patch of hay. It was a beautiful scene, except for the fact that Zaza kept kicking and farting and eating every bit of fruit in the manger throughout the mass. It was embarrassing for us, as Zaza's keepers, to watch her behave so badly, but I noticed that for everyone else, it didn't really matter. All that mattered was that the midnight mass brought just about every person in the village together to celebrate their faith in God, from the very youngest (our star performer) to the very oldest. And it wasn't just at Christmas— every Sunday mass drew worshippers from every part of the village. It was remarkable to see the power of a simple church to unite people this way.

Along with that for me, however, came the particularly Catholic fear of doing something wrong. Not sinning, necessarily, but just messing up a ritual, or being inadvertently blasphemous. That was enforced during my time at Ampleforth boarding school, on the grounds of a Catholic Benedictine monastery. There our schedule of worship was rigid and intense—mass five times a week, prayers twice a day, twice-weekly benedictions. The rituals were nonstop. For the benedictions, a few dozen of us would be led down into a windowless, airless crypt, where we stood motionless side by side for hours, trying to avoid the heavy incense smoke wafting around us. Boys would occasionally collapse under the strain and get carried away while the benediction continued uninterrupted. I assume we were meant to learn the value of sacrifice and devotion, but at the time it seemed an odd form of hardship to be endured, which we all took to be just another part of what it meant to be a good Christian.

If fear, to me, was a key facet of Catholicism, its sometimes sister principle was guilt. When I was young, I felt guilty about all sorts of transgressions. At Ampleforth, a housemate and I learned where the priests kept the holy wine and, one night, snuck up to the rafters of a big storage room in the monastery where barrels of wine were stored. We opened one and enjoyed a few sips. Almost immediately after we left, I felt terrible guilt about what I'd done. I honestly thought I'd been drinking the literal blood of Christ just for kicks, and the enormity of that blasphemy was crushing. Eventually I learned the wine needs to be consecrated before it becomes the blood of Christ, which lessened the guilt, but only a bit.

I remember another time when I was a teenager and prayed to God to help me win a tennis match. I didn't win, and afterward I was furious, first with God for not helping me prevail, but then also with myself for invoking God's name for such a frivolous reason. The guilt I felt served as a guardrail, keeping me in the proper bounds of Catholicism.

In my twenties, and especially after I became a war correspondent, I became more questioning of my faith.

Some of that was inevitable. As we grow up and move on to college and encounter people of different faiths, it's natural to question the beliefs instilled in us when we were young. Which parts of those teachings do we want to keep, and which are we okay with letting go? When I began covering the wars in Iraq and Afghanistan and Syria—conflicts that in large part were about religious devotion, or what many would call religious fanaticism—I saw up close the unthinkable atrocities people committed in the name of their God, Allah. In Aleppo, where my friend Rick Findler and I traveled with a band of Syrian rebels fighting against the Assad regime, we watched rebels launch homemade grenades from a catapult and cry *Takbir* or *Allahu akbar*—God is greater than all—with every launch. We had to say it too, because our silence would have offended the rebels.

Death and destruction hand in hand with fervent devotion to God—this was the reality of so many of those wars and many others around the world too. People invoking God to wreak havoc and destroy life? Surely their religion had gotten it all wrong. Another time, Rick and I were sitting with a rebel fighter who asked us if we were Christians. I answered that I was, but Rick said he didn't believe in any god. The rebel fighter grew furious. "Never say that," he sternly warned us. "Never say you don't believe in God. They will kill you." Being Christian in a Muslim land was tolerable to some, but not believing in God at all was totally blasphemous and could very well get you killed.

Likewise, I saw Christians turning to God to get them through the horrors of war. In Iraq, I covered a Christian militia fighting against ISIS, which wanted to eradicate Christianity altogether. I learned about a church that ISIS had bombed and reduced to near-rubble, save for the altar and a big crucifix, which, somehow, still stood tall and untouched. The local priest continued to say mass amid the rubble and wished to rebuild his church and community. When I heard about this, I knew it was a story I wanted to cover. Getting to the church wasn't easy. ISIS laid mines all over the fields surrounding it, and we had to creep slowly and build a safe zigzag path to the demolished church.

Once there, I was astonished by what I saw. The destruction was all but complete, the bombs leveling everything except for a sliver of wall on which hung a large plain crucifix. Literally everything in the church had crumbled down around it, yet there it was, defiant, miraculous, in place in front of the equally untouched altar. And there we Christians gathered to pray, missiles crashing in the distance. The image of the indestructible cross was a stunning symbol of the power of faith, the power of God, to see us through dark times.

I could not deny that God's influence on His believers was real and profound and richly positive. At the same time, neither could I deny the butchery and depravity of people fighting for the way they saw *their* god. Here was that challenging duality again: Did religious fervor help people survive wars, or did it cause them in the first place? Was religion being used by some to motivate believers to commit atrocities? Or was religion only a force for good in the world? One thing about seeing war up close is that it disavows you of the notion that any one truth is correct. Every side is convinced of the rightness of their cause. It seemed to me that both good and evil were part of the dual reality of religious devotion. It wasn't as simple as saying prayers in a crypt or chanting in a monastery. It was complex. Faith was a battleground, constantly tested and challenged, and we all had to find our own bit of wall that remained standing in the smoke and ash and rubble.

Covering wars for fifteen years changed my relationship with God. It went from being consistently questioning to being more of an on-and-off thing. There were times after witnessing truly inhuman brutality that I questioned if God existed at all, or if there was a heaven, or if my God was the only God. There were times when I spoke openly to God and asked for advice, and other times when I thought the existence of God didn't matter, because I believed we should all strive to behave a certain way based on our inherent moral integrity and not on any book or teaching. I still appreciated the many positives of steeping yourself in your faith, but I also had questions about how other faiths had descended into religious zealotry. My relationship with God was, more than anything, an ongoing conversation, a back-and-forth. Was I doing enough for God and other people to qualify as a good Christian? Or did it even matter if I was or wasn't?

Then—a bomb fell on me in Ukraine.

The questions I now had to ask myself were different and even more complex—was it God who saved me on that day? And did I want God and religion to be my path through the long, painful recovery ahead?

* * *

At BAMC, Jock and I did not enter the chapel that first day out of the ward. We didn't go on our second outing either. It took me about two months to finally go, and that was only because there was a long line outside the canteen. I thought about Pierre, as I did pretty much every day, and this time I got the feeling that I really ought to go into that chapel, and talk to Pierre in there, and maybe say a prayer for him too. *Come on already, just go in*, I could almost hear him say. *What are you waiting for? Just go.*

So, I did. Jock wheeled me through the entrance doors and into a small, darkened room with a high vaulted ceiling. There were five or six rows of wooden pews on either side of a central aisle, and in front a raised platform with a simple altar, a small podium, and the American flag. Behind the altar was a rectangular stained-glass window featuring an insignia and the Latin words *Pro Deo Et Patria*—the Army chaplain motto meaning *For God and Country*.

Immediately, I felt unusually calm. I was no longer in a hospital, or even a wheelchair—I was in an uncommonly quiet, peaceful, reflective space that made me someone different from the person who came in. I felt this way whenever I entered a church or a chapel, which I often did in London just to escape the bustle and noise of city life. But in this chapel, the sense of removal from the physical world was even more intense.

The chapel was empty except for us and one woman in the back row praying quietly. I wondered who she was praying for. Someone who was injured but alive, like me, or someone she had lost? I thought of all the thousands of people who had come through those doors before me, bringing with them unfathomable pain and suffering and heartbreak. I remembered that this was where Sarah Verardo, who put together the team that rescued me from Ukraine, prayed for me when she visited BAMC. It was where she prayed for her own husband years earlier, after he was left broken by a bombing just like I was. All those prayers, said humbly in these pews, carried with them the hopes and dreams of husbands and wives, mothers and fathers, families and communities, reaching out to God in their darkest hour.

I understood I was in a special place.

Up near the front of the chapel, I saw an Army chaplain, one of four who traded long, around-the-clock shifts at BAMC. I asked Jock to wheel me over. Perhaps because of my upbringing I've always enjoyed talking to priests. I find them to be fascinating characters. The enormous sacrifice they chose to make—giving up their lives for something bigger than themselves—leaves me in something like awe. Priests, in my experience, were engaging to talk to and almost always helpful with whatever problem you brought them. And to bear the weight of all that suffering placed on their shoulders? These were strong, resilient servants of God and I admired them.

The Army chaplain, William Breckenridge, greeted me with a warm smile. I told him my name and what happened.

"I was in Ukraine and I wanted to come down and, you know, say a prayer for my colleagues who didn't make it out, and I want to talk to them to tell them what I would have told them that day, and let them know how much I miss them."

The chaplain joined me in saying a prayer for Pierre and for our young Ukrainian fixer, Sasha, and for the two brave Ukrainian soldiers who also died in that car. Jock set my wheelchair at the end of a pew, and we sat there for the next half hour, each of us praying quietly. I often spoke to Pierre in my hospital room, but now, in the chapel, it felt like I had a more direct connection to him. I told him I was working extremely hard on my recovery as a way to honor him, because I knew he would want to see me back on my feet and out in the world again, pursuing the kinds of adventures that thrilled us both so much. I promised Pierre I wouldn't let up until I walked back into Ukraine under my own power, and not even then. I told Pierre how greatly he was missed.

Then it felt as if Pierre was talking back to me, telling me I could do it, and do it with a smile on my face, just as he always, always had on his. In this moment, I felt I'd been given permission to allow my Christianity to play a part in my recovery, in the reconstruction of me, and this was a deeply welcoming feeling, because at the time I needed all the help I could get.

The truth is that I felt more open to that possibility the moment I entered the chapel. Feeling like you are part of something much, much bigger than yourself is both comforting and empowering, because it is so much easier to go through a trauma with someone else than all by yourself. And if I had forgotten that I was never alone, not even in that deserted village outside Kyiv when all four of my colleagues were gone and my own survival seemed impossible, being in that chapel reminded me that no matter where I was, I was still a part of another community—the community of people whose belief in God meant they never had to go through any hardship alone.

In that small, quiet chapel, I said a prayer to God and asked for His help.

I need you by my side, I said. *I need you to help keep me moving forward. Because what I want to do, what I need to do, is get back to my family, to my wife and children. That's all I want. And I know how much family means to you, so, whatever help you can give me, I would be grateful.*

It all made more sense to me after that visit to the chapel. It was okay that I was questioning God, but why not ask for His help at the same time? What was the risk of asking God to pitch in? I was relying on my work ethic and my resiliency to get me through the recovery process, and also on the love of my family and children, but what was the harm of layering God's help on top of all that? Even if I wasn't sure I believed in God's healing grace or not, why would I turn my back on it in such a desperate time? Why not welcome it with love and reverence?

I went back to the chapel several more times during my stay at BAMC, and even after I was transferred to the nearby unit that worked on my prosthetics. Every time, I felt that peace and serenity again. I felt my concerns fall away, like the roof and walls of that church in Iraq fell away, leaving only an altar and a crucifix. All I was left with, I realized, was one simple, powerful thing:

A conversation between God and me.

*   *   *

After I made it home to London and my family, I placed a call to one of the Army chaplains I'd spoken with at BAMC in Texas. His name is Chaplain Steve Glenn. He was a Navy diver before he became a chaplain, and he was an exceedingly kind, gentle, and thoughtful man. I told him I had some questions about grief and God and resilience and faith, and he said he was happy to talk. At BAMC, he counseled hundreds of injured soldiers and their families, gradually gaining their trust and steering them back to God, often after they had strongly turned away from Him before.

"At some point in their lives they were convinced there was something bigger than themselves out there, but after what happened to them they're not really sure what that something is anymore," Father Glenn told me. I understood what he was saying. My Catholic upbringing had always made me feel like I was part of something bigger, and even just being in the chapel at BAMC made me feel that way. But I wasn't always sure what that something was. God? Family? Community? Humanity? Faith? The bombing in Ukraine only made me more questioning about my relationship with God, and the fragility of life, and what it all meant.

I never once consciously asked myself, "Why did this have to happen to me?" I never, ever saw myself as a victim or complained that life is unfair. I just don't think that way; I know how blessed I am. But I guess I did question what, besides my right leg and left foot, had been lost in the bombing. Yes, I had been saved, but what was gone forever? Were parts of me irretrievably lost? Was I the same person I was before the bombing?

Father Glenn jumped right in. "Today, you might not feel like you were gifted anything, but rather that something was taken away," he said in a measured tone. "But your abilities and talents were all instilled through God's design, and those gifts, those talents, still reside in you. Your physical abilities may have changed, but the gifts God gave you have not. *Those gifts cannot be taken away*."

Well, what about those who had lost all faith? Who'd gone through such devastating trauma they no longer believed God could help them? Who may even feel God *did* forsake them? What hope is there for them? Father Glenn believes that some of that extreme doubt could derive from fear. "In times like these I see people having a continual dialogue with fear," he said. "This is a fear they may have to walk with for the rest of their lives. Ideally, there is a process of not letting the fear control you and moving it away from right in front of you to your side, because if it stays in your eyeline you won't ever see the horizon. The fear becomes an anchor that holds you back."

That made sense to me. We all have fears and doubts, and we may have to live with some of them forever. But it's possible to move them to the side and press ahead anyway. Courage, it's been said, is not the absence of fear. It's doing what you need to do in *spite* of the fear. As a journalist, I prided myself on being able to push past fear and do whatever was needed to get a story. I ran down a bombed-out street as snipers' bullets narrowly missed me; I had a rifle held to my temple but never lost my cool or nerve. I believed I'd learned to control my fears and not let them hold me back.

But now, after the bombing, the nature of my fear had changed. I wasn't frightened of terrorists or land mines or sneak attacks. What I thought about instead was my new life, and what it was going to look like.

"That part of the struggle can be truly terrifying for some people," Father Glenn said. "What's terrifying is having to accept their changed lives. But the spiritual side of it can also be frightening, because suddenly you are engaging God in a way you've never had to engage Him before."

Father Glenn asked about my spiritual condition, and what part God was playing in my recovery. I told him my relationship with God was a questioning one, a constant dialogue, with moments when I asked for His help and others when I wasn't sure He was there. I appreciated the positives of faith and the beauty of God's creations, but I had also seen the very worst of human nature, and reconciling the two was a struggle. Father Glenn had heard this before.

"A lot of people who I see at BAMC have probably just experienced the worst moment of their lives, and it's a good possibility that they are angry at God," he said. "They're going to be mad at me too, because I represent God. Sometimes, someone will tell me to get out of their room; they don't want me there. I understand how they feel, and I know I'll have to have some very hard conversations with them and their families. But I have to get past the anger first."

So how does he do that?

"It's about building trust and assuring them of God's support. And reminding them that running to God with their anger is a whole lot better than running away from God. Because if you run away from God, you will feel alone."

Those words resonated with me. The feeling of not being alone in my journey of recovery. I felt it when I walked into the chapel at BAMC and saw a lone woman praying in a back pew. I saw her and I thought, *It's not just you. It's not just you. So many people have been on this same journey and walked through those very doors and sat there and prayed, just like you. It's not just you. You aren't alone. You are part of something bigger.*

What this meant to me was that I hadn't rejected God. I wasn't angry with Him and I didn't want to cut off communication. I still questioned Him, but that was all right, because in my questioning I didn't run away from Him. My questions were *for* Him, not about Him.

* * *

This book is about staying resolute in the face of great adversity. Staying purposeful, determined, unwavering. My conversation with Father Glenn convinced me that part of being resolute is not being too pigheaded. As singular and solitary as your journey may seem to you, as mine did to me, believing we can accomplish our goals without any help from anyone can lead to arrogance and be detrimental. No matter who or what or where we are, we are all part of something bigger than ourselves, and we all owe something to someone.

My thoughts about this start with the realization that I didn't get on this earth by myself. I was not responsible for my creation, and I am in debt to someone or something. This debt, however, is not a negative thing. In fact, it's a very positive thing. It is what binds us to the larger community of humanity, and to each other. We're all on this journey together, which means we are never alone.

Okay, but then what about Horenka? Where was God when those Russian missiles landed on us in a village that had already been destroyed? Why did everyone in that car perish except me? If I was questioning about God before such a senseless tragedy killed so many good people, how could I not be even more questioning now? Or did God's seeming absence in Horenka answer my questions once and for all?

I wrestled with this for a long time after the bombing. But now I've had time to go back over everything that happened in Ukraine and piece together a narrative that made at least some sense to me, like a journalist reconstructing a crime. I realized that, in fact, God *was* there with me in Horenka. Because when everything else fell away, when precious little hope remained, when my world went black and I lost all sensation and brushed the very edges of death, the thing I instinctively returned to when I opened my eyes and squinted against the smoke and ash was this—family and God.

I thought back hard on that very moment when I awoke on the asphalt in pieces, and I tried to confirm the first thoughts I had. I remembered it all. First, I noticed I was alive. Then I saw my right leg was missing. I understood I was gravely injured and in the middle of nowhere. I called out to Pierre, and then I thought about Alicia and the girls. I told myself that no matter what, I was getting back to them.

Then, instinctively and without forethought, I offered a prayer to God:

Get me home. Please help me get home.

There it was. *God, I need You.* All the Hail Marys and Our Fathers at Ampleforth, all the Bible lessons and Gregorian chants and visits to the crypt, all the exhortations to trust and honor and obey, all the one-on-one conversations with God I'd had over nearly forty years—all of that led me back to the simplest, purest prayer: *God, get me home.*

Perhaps I would never stop questioning. But when it mattered, I knew that I was not alone in Horenka.

I named my first book *Saved* because I wanted to honor the heroism of the people who kept me from dying and got me out of Ukraine, of the U.S. Army soldiers who whisked me to America and patched me up, and of those who didn't survive but live on in me and others. *Saved*, it seemed, was a very appropriate title for a book about a man whose life was spared.

But was that all that "saved" meant to me?

Had I, on that day in Horenka, been saved by God?

As a journalist it's my job to find the facts, not draw conclusions. I also know it is part of my nature to always question everything, and I know my relationship with God will remain a questioning one. But I also know that is okay. The important thing is that I did not turn away from my faith, even on the darkest day of my life. Quite the opposite—I reached out for it. We don't have to have the answers to every question we raise, about the existence of both good and evil in the world, about the downside of religious fervency, about the role God plays in our lives. It's likely that we'll never have all those answers.

What I have learned, however, is that part of what it means to be resolute is being resolute in our beliefs as well.

*   *   *

Before the bombing, I often said prayers while I was in war zones—not formal prayers but rather little pleas for guidance and safety. Not just for myself, but for my colleagues and the soldiers. These pleadings usually came in the form of a Bible verse. Since the bombing I've forgotten many of the things I used to say in those moments. But there is one verse I still remember today.

It's from Psalm 23:

The LORD is my shepherd; I shall not want.
He makes me lie down in green pastures.
He leads me beside still waters.
He restores my soul.

He leads me in paths of righteousness
for his name's sake.
Even though I walk through the valley of the
shadow of death, I will fear no evil,
for you are with me.

13

HAZARD

Spring 2024

TOWN OF HAZARD

Perry County, Eastern Kentucky

s much as I longed to return to places like Ukraine and Israel and cover global conflicts again, part of me wanted to try something else. After nearly two decades of visiting the world's most hellish hot spots, I felt the need tell a different kind of story—not just about turmoil and hatred and violence, but instead about *resilience and recovery*.

I knew from experience that the media tends to devote tons of resources to covering conflicts and far fewer to follow-up stories about rebuilding, rejuvenation, and optimism. That is just the nature of the news business. But in the last two years I've learned that the aftermath of tragedy, the long, lonely battle to heal and find meaning again, is every bit as dramatic—and brutally challenging—as the initial tragedy. Sometimes what happens *after* the cameras shut off is the real story you're looking for.

So, I pitched Fox News on the idea of a series of reports about people and places that exemplified this spirit of resilience and perseverance—a series I called *American Exceptionalism*. After everything I'd been through, and was still going through, I felt like I could relate to other people who'd met unlucky fates and refused to buckle under the weight of their hardships, and who instead chose to fight and come back stronger. This was my mindset, and I wanted to report on others who approached their lives the same way. I wanted to better understand and showcase the transformative power of resilience.

Fox News liked the idea and sent me out to find the best subject for the report. After some research, we discovered the perfect place. It was a small American town that in the last thirty years suffered one devastating setback after another, ravaging the place and turning it into a tragic national symbol of loss, desperation, and failure. That, of course, was only the beginning of the story. Much more newsworthy to me was what happened next.

*   *   *

In the spring of 2024, a few weeks after I'd returned from Israel, I went to New York City to attend to some Fox News business, and from there I took a two-hour flight south to Lexington, Kentucky—the heart of Appalachia country.

Appalachia is a distinct geographic and cultural region defined by the sprawling, multistate Appalachian Mountain range in the eastern United States. From Lexington we drove another two hours to the small town of Hazard, about one hundred miles north of the

Tennessee border and against the north fork of the Kentucky River. The drive to Hazard along Kentucky Highway 9006 is scenic and winding, through valleys and up and down hills framed by sweeping mountains. The town itself is small enough to drive past if you're not paying attention—some 5,500 people on just seven square miles. But once you're there you can almost feel the weight of its past. That's because, for a century, you could describe it in just two words: coal town.

Coal is what turned the U.S. into an industrial superpower, and the first American coal was wrenched from the Appalachian Mountains, initially in Pennsylvania and then—after railroads connected eastern Kentucky to the industrialized world in the early 1900s—in hundreds of towns near coal mines like Hazard. Kentucky alone has pulled nearly ten billion tons of coal from its mines since 1790, more than in all but three other U.S. states.

Hazard was in the middle of it all, sitting between the Algoma and Black Gold coal companies. The mines employed generations of townspeople and provided them with good, stable livings. "My grandfather worked in the deep mines and would come home completely black with coal dust," the charming, garrulous mayor of Hazard, Donald "Happy" Mobelini, one of the first people I spoke with when I arrived in Hazard, told me. "We had a big brush and when I was six we'd go out and scrub his back. That's just what you did. But he made good money, and everybody you knew worked in the coal mines at one time."

Scott Alexander, another Hazard resident I sat and spoke with, told me, "The working conditions were tough, but the men were tougher."

The coal mines created prosperity, community, continuity, friendships, families. The mines weren't just part of an industry;

they were a way of life. The miners of Kentucky helped the U.S. win World War I, and then World War II, and the miners of Hazard helped each other through crises, attended each other's weddings, celebrated births and graduations together. Hazard was coal, and coal was Hazard, and that worked well for thousands of families for a long time.

But then, in the 1980s, the United States began moving away from coal.

That was the first devastating blow for Hazard. When greater awareness of global warming and the push toward renewable energy sharply cut the demand for coal, the economic heart of Hazard stopped beating. Mines closed and jobs went away, and no other industries arrived to fill the gap. Small, remote towns like Hazard saw stores boarded up, buildings condemned, and schools closed, as more and more townspeople fled in search of better opportunities elsewhere. Once lively downtowns vanished. In this way, a thriving, close-knit community like Hazard became a shell of itself, still standing but greatly diminished, its future a question mark.

"We became a ghost town it seemed overnight," Happy explained. "You can't find anybody that lives in eastern Kentucky who didn't have some parent, grandparent, aunt, uncle, somebody that worked for the coal industry. You take that away and you've got a depressed area."

Hazard's vulnerability opened it up to a second devastating blow—the opioid crisis.

Starting in the late 1990s, the overuse or misuse of prescription opioid painkillers such as oxycodone, hydrocodone, and fentanyl caused a massive spike in addictions and overdose deaths across the U.S. (the number of OD deaths nearly quadrupled from 8.2 per 100,000 people in 2002 to 32.6 in 2022). Accidental OD deaths—

caused primarily by the powerful synthetic painkiller fentanyl—
surged, increasing an astonishing 622 percent in twenty years. In
some states, opioid fatalities more than doubled the number of
deaths in vehicle accidents.

The epicenter of this crisis was Appalachia. The heavy labor of coal
mining led many to a dependency on painkillers that only worsened
as opioids became more addictive and more available. Rural states
like Kentucky and West Virginia were particularly hard hit, as pain
mills—loosely supervised medical clinics—popped up in every mall,
freely dispensing what some called hillbilly heroin.

At one point, four counties in eastern Kentucky led the nation in
opioid hospitalization rates, with Perry County, home to Hazard, the
single hardest-hit county in the U.S. "Around my junior year in high
school we started seeing an influx of opioids in the region," Hazard
resident Mandi Fugate Sheffel, a recovering addict, told me. "I would
go to parties and there would be pills. And then OxyContin in
particular, I think, was the real shift for me."

Along the way, Hazard fought back. People kicked addictions,
new stores opened here and there. But the bad luck continued.
In 2020 and 2022, historically heavy rainfall caused deadly river
overflows and flash flooding that left towns like Hazard practically
underwater. Some homes were flooded; others were yanked from
their foundations and swept away by the powerful currents. And
then, just as some businesses were heroically struggling to reopen,
came the Covid pandemic, which shuttered any stores that survived
the floods.

Pummeled by this series of catastrophes, Hazard could have gone
either way. "I lost many people to addiction, many friends and family
members, and it's devastating, but it does either one thing or another,"

Jenny Combs, one of many Hazard residents I spoke with, told me. "It devastates you to the point where you just want to give up. Or—it fuels your passion to help those who are still alive."

Hazard, it seemed, wasn't done yet.

*   *   *

My Fox News team and I drove the final leg of our trip to Hazard through beautiful forests and over winding scenic roads. The towns-people there immediately treated us like relatives who'd finally come to pay a visit. I'm not sure if I've ever met a friendlier group of people anywhere in the world, despite all of the uncommonly tough times they'd endured.

Sometimes, it's those who've been through the worst and somehow survived who become the most powerful agents for change. In Hazard, that was the case with people like Stephanie Callahan. Over coffee, Stephanie told me the story of her life. When she was younger, Stephanie was addicted to OxyContin and bounced in and out of rehab centers, never quite straightening herself out. She spent three years in one rehab clinic in a neighboring county, "but then as soon as I hit the county line my car was in overdrive to the dope dealers. It was insane."

Then Stephanie learned she was pregnant. She'd always wanted to be a mother, but when it was finally happening, she was still caught up in her addiction. "The doctor told me, 'You're going to have to get straight or we're going to take the baby,'" Stephanie said. "And I'm like, 'No, you're not taking my baby. I'm not losing him. I prayed for him, so, all right, it's time to do this.'"

Stephanie kicked her addiction and had her baby, and she's been clean ever since. When her hometown of Hazard hit rock bottom, just as she had, she believed she had to do something about it. Against the odds, and smack in the middle of the Covid pandemic, she opened her own clothing store in downtown Hazard. She called it the Hot Mess Express, "because, you know, I'm a hot mess." People told her she'd lost her mind. But the opportunity was there—before her shop, women like her had to drive two hours to buy plus-sized clothing in Lexington—and so was the dream.

Just three years later, Stephanie's small clothing empire is not only surviving but thriving—she has nine part-time employees *and* plans to open another clothing store for men.

She wasn't the only one in Hazard to defy the odds. Several others had stories similar to hers. For instance, Mandi Fugate Sheffel, who overcame her own addiction to pills, opened a small bookstore on Main Street called the Read Spotted Newt.

In fact, in the last handful of years, around fifty new businesses have opened in Hazard, among them a smoothie shop, a toy store, a café, and a restaurant. This business boom has created nearly two hundred jobs, many of which went to former addicts who got clean.

I spoke to many citizens of Hazard who told me similar stories. Corey Shockey, a longtime Hazard resident, says she was addicted to painkillers for twenty-five years. "My parents were addicts too," she said. "They made a way of life out of it. I was raised around it and it was always normal to me."

Susan Brotherton, Corey's boss at a pantry shelf, remembers her from those days. "I had to fire her one night in our parking lot," Susan told me. "She had some problems and her life was out of control. She couldn't function or work."

Nevertheless, when Corey got clean in 2018 after finally entering rehab, Susan decided to give her another chance. "I came into work one day and some of the employees who remembered her said she'd been by and she looked great and she was clean," said Susan. "And I said, 'Well, call her, because I loved her before.' We hired her back and all she's done is rise up. She manages my stores and makes me all kinds of money. And she does it for herself too."

I asked Corey where she found the strengthen to finally kick her addiction, which had seemed insurmountable for so long. "I just started seeing how other people were doing so much better and feeling better," she told me. "They were always in good moods. I admired that and that's what I wanted. So that's what I did."

The more I spoke with townspeople, the more I realized that none of these success stories were isolated. They were all part of a much bigger story—a story of community. Recovered addicts inspiring recovering addicts, new store owners inspiring would-be entrepreneurs. Case by case, store by store, they all brought new life to Hazard, and with each new burst of hope in the town came another success, another dream fulfilled. "We were on top of the world at one time," the mayor explained. "Then we lost coal and we went to the bottom of the world. But now, we're coming back."

*   *   *

As a journalist, I've traveled all over the world, been to some remarkable places, and met the most fascinating people you'd ever want to meet. I have seen ordinary people confront impossible odds and tap into some hidden strength they didn't even know was there and find a way to get through the hell of their situation. I have seen just how resilient and defiant human beings can be, in the face of the most inhuman atrocities and injustices you can imagine.

Yet there was something about Hazard and the people who live there that just blew me away. Perhaps it was because of what I'd gone through, and was still going through, that I found the citizens of Hazard so uniquely inspirational. Perhaps I likened their resiliency to my own—how they hit rock bottom, seemingly had no way out, and somehow managed to rise up, anyway. Whatever it was, I can honestly say I've never been more impressed with a group of people than I was with the folks in Hazard.

When I was there, I took the opportunity to drive around the town just to meet with and talk to people. I sat with one older man confined to a wheelchair who told me about what the town did for him during one of the major floods. He lived in a tiny house in the middle of the woods and the flooding wiped out the road he used to come and go. Marooned inside, he didn't call anyone for help, but he didn't have to—the people in his community already knew he was someone they had to look after. And so, on their own, a group of them set out for his house on their dirt-diggers and cleared the road for him. A bunch of local high school kids also pitched in. It was a beautiful example of what a community can accomplish when it comes together around a common cause.

It was resilience in action.

No one in Hazard embodies this more than Mayor Happy.

He's been called Happy his whole life because when he was born someone picked him up and said, "This is the happiest baby ever," and the name stuck. Happy drove me around Hazard one day, and it was like being in a car with a celebrity. Everywhere we went, people knew him and either waved hello as we drove by or shouted out some business they had with him.

"I'm finally hooking up that water pipe," one person hollered as we slowed up alongside him.

"Great, give Steve a call, he'll make sure you get those screws and get it running by tomorrow."

"Hey, Happy, I'm getting in the order for an extra car for the fire station," another man yelled out a block later.

"Okay, I'm gonna call the estate and get a cheap one," Happy answered. "We'll get it on the cheap."

Then we drove around some of the still-depressed areas of Hazard so Happy could describe his plans for them.

"We're gonna fix that playground," he said, pointing at a run-down area. "They're gonna come tomorrow and fix it."

A few blocks later: "We've gotta fix up that parking lot there and get a big parking lot. Now we got all these businesses coming downtown and they need parking."

Minutes later: "We've got a project to build a big sports facility with tennis courts, baseball fields, all of it."

Happy's energy was infectious and inspiring. Like me, he is someone who can't sit still for a minute. Every Christmas, for instance, Happy visits children who have been orphaned because their parents succumbed to their drug addictions and gives each one a gift he made himself. He also drives around town looking for homeless kids and gets them motel rooms. He is like one of those folksy heroes you see in movies about small but magical towns. Happy is even helping the incarcerated turn around their lives.

"We have some really cool programs going on in the jail," he told me excitedly. "We're transporting prisoners to the community college at night, and to vocational schools, and they're getting certificates."

The other target group for Mayor Happy and others like him in Hazard are people who don't even drive yet.

One of the many places I visited while I was there was a beautiful little baseball field nestled in the mountains and forests—home to Hazard's high school baseball team. We stood for the national anthem, cheered when anyone got a hit or made a great play, and just reveled in the atmosphere of wholesomeness. I was struck by the power of such a simple ritual, by the meaningfulness of seeing these boys and girls proudly wearing the name Hazard on their jerseys, and by the sheer gratitude of their parents watching and cheering from the stands. There was a sense of permanence and tradition about the event, as if it had always been there, and always would be in the future. As if it was something that *mattered*.

To break century-long cycles of generational poverty and addiction, the grown-ups of Hazard know they will have to make sure their children stick around. "The stereotype has always been that if you really want to get anywhere big-time you have to leave Hazard," Stephanie Callahan said. But now the people of Hazard are proving you can be successful there and take advantage of everything else it offers—tradition, community, friendship, family, and pride in one's hometown.

"I want to make Hazard the best place there is," Terry Davidson, a native of the town, told me. "When I get older, I want to bring my kids around town and tell them that I helped bring our community back after coal. I was part of it."

"This town has so much potential," a resident named Chelsea Stacy told me. "And I feel like if we can get the future generations to be a part of it, this could be something very, very special."

* * *

The truth is, Hazard is already a very special place.

I've been in many towns and villages all over the world that have been crushed by tragedy and reduced to shells of their former selves. But because I've always moved on to the next war someplace else, I never really got the chance to see how those towns and villages fared once the conflict was over. Did they rebuild? Did everyone just flee? Did these once-thriving communities simply cease to exist?

In my trip to Hazard, Kentucky, I finally got to see just that—a once-battered town *reinventing itself*.

Two things about my time in Hazard stood out. One was the strong sense of community—one of the keys to overcoming adversity that I had witnessed, and experienced, time and time again in my travels. Hazard was a brilliant example of why that is true. Helping each other out of troubling spots comes naturally to its residents, as if it were built into the bedrock of the town.

The other thing that really stayed with me was how much of Hazard's spectacular reinvention is being powered by the very people who used to be its biggest problem.

The theme of broken people finding a way to endure and come back from the depths was obviously significant for me. All the ideas about resilience that I've been thinking about and trying to put into practice were fully on display in Hazard, not just in one person but in *every* person—and especially in those who overcame drug addictions.

In some ways I felt a kinship with the people of Hazard—people who rose up out of what surely seemed to them to be an inescapable pit. Perhaps, like me, they'd even felt death itself hovering around them when they were at their worst and weakest. Yet here they were, having fought and clawed their way back to life, not just the same as they used to be but better than they ever were. Stronger, wiser, happier, more capable. They had refused to become just another statistic—one of the more than 100,000 people in the U.S. who die of drug overdoses every year. Instead they became the best versions of themselves they could be.

The people of Hazard helped me understand that resilience—the process of adapting to difficult and challenging new life experiences—

goes hand in hand with reinvention, our ability to transform ourselves in response to the new demands of our lives.

After I left Hazard and went home to London, I researched the historic adaptability of human beings and came across this quote by NASA astrobiologist David Grinspoon, a prominent speaker on the subject. "We are unique in our capacity for reinvention," Grinspoon said in one of his talks. "In times of existential threat, we have completely reinvented ourselves before."

Prehumans, for instance, were hunter-gatherers until the Ice Age wiped out any game to hunt. In response, the species developed new methods and tools for pulling up shellfish and managed to survive. "There are many examples of where, when faced with catastrophe, we reinvented ourselves," Grinspoon says. "That's what we humans are good at."

I was inspired by the people of Hazard as they, like me, continue the process of defining and creating their new lives. I think anyone who faces adversity can and should draw inspiration from their story. Hazard was all but written off as a cautionary tale, an example of how a group of people were decimated by societal changes they couldn't control.

Yet the people of Hazard refused to go along with that narrative. They ignored the long odds against them pulling off any kind of a turnaround. As one resident put it, "It was David versus Goliath, and no one thought we could win but us." No savior swooped in to save them; no twist of fate or fortune paved their way. Instead they just buckled down and, as Appalachians tend to do, they handled things themselves.

As Mayor Happy phrased it: "There's nothing wrong with having a problem. It's how you fight your way out of it, you know?"

14

BREATHE

Everywhere, Every Day

There are moments in my life now when something happens and all I can do is laugh.

Not long ago, I went for a drive in London in my hand-controlled car. I parked by the sidewalk and opened the door to step out and get on with things. But just as I did, my right leg fell apart and broke off at the knee and spilled out of the car. One minute I was my new, independent self, running an errand on my own, resuming my somewhat normal life. The next I was stranded legless in my car with no way of reattaching my prosthetic. It wasn't a major problem: I was testing out a new prosthetic and it hadn't been properly attached during the trial, so all I had to do was turn around and drive back home and wait for someone to get back so they could pass me a spare leg from the house. No big deal.

It was, however, a reminder that my life had changed in irrevocable ways. And it was humbling. Even so, I didn't allow myself to feel dejected or frustrated; instead, I saw the humor in it. I imagined someone passing by and seeing my leg hop out of the car a few seconds before I did, and wondering what the heck was going on.

That is where I am today: somewhere between who I was and who I'll eventually be. Or maybe we never really become a set, fully defined person, and life is all a journey, in which case I'm at some point on the road, steadily moving forward. One of the reasons I was so excited to write this book was that it was a way for me to figure out just who the new me is. A truly seismic event interrupted my life, and knocked me off my chosen course, and as much as I may have wanted to return to the person I used to be, I understood I was already someone very different. I also realized there would be a steep and lengthy learning curve, along which I would need to constantly adapt and readapt and try new things and slowly settle into something like my new life.

It's been a step-by-step process, accepting, adapting, embracing, aspiring, reinventing, and so on. I'm sure there will be many more steps I need to take, and eventually I'll become a sort of pseudo-expert on trauma and recovery. Now, the last thing I ever thought would happen was that the story of my life would be an inspiration to anyone. I sometimes thought my work as a journalist might enlighten people, but my life? No. As a journalist I was careful to not insert myself into my stories, to remain invisible. But then I found that people were curious about what I'd gone through, and some even found it easier to talk to me about their challenges than to anyone else because of what I'd experienced. And I realized if there was any chance I could help anyone overcome adversity in their lives, I had to embrace that and do whatever I could to have an impact.

In my research into how we humans react to trauma and adversity, I came across a concept in psychology known as post-traumatic growth. PTG refers to the phenomenon of major crises and traumatic events having a positive psychological effect on those who experience them. As *Psychology Today* put it, "Post-Traumatic Growth doesn't deny deep distress, but rather posits that adversity can unintentionally yield changes in understanding oneself, others and the world." The psychologists who named the phenomenon in the 1990s identified five areas of potential post-trauma growth:

- Recognizing and embracing new opportunities;
- Forging stronger relationships with loved ones;
- Cultivating inner strength through the knowledge of having overcome tremendous hardship;
- Gaining a deeper appreciation for life;
- Discovering new depths of faith and spirituality.

These positive changes might not seem possible in the immediate aftermath of the trauma. The more natural reaction is to believe that nothing good can ever come from what happened, that it's a meaningless tragedy and that it has destroyed our lives. But research has shown otherwise. The *Harvard Business Review* reported that, in time, "negative experiences can spur positive change. We see this in people who have endured war, natural disasters, bereavement, job loss, economic stress and serious illness and injuries."

The research shows exactly what I had been experiencing in the aftermath of the bombing, in the long months of my recovery, and, I'm sure, in the years to come: trauma disrupts our core belief systems, forcing us to rethink our place in the world, our future, ourselves. These deep, uninvited questions—*Who am I? What matters to me now? What kind of world do I live in?*—can be painful to contemplate. But they can also lead to changes that are undeniably valuable and positive. For example, in the same *Harvard Business Review* report, it was found that "people are often surprised by how well they have handled trauma." As a result, "they are left better equipped to tackle future challenges." Overcoming adversity can't help but make you stronger. What's more, victims of trauma can cultivate this post-traumatic growth by shifting their mindsets away from negatives that are easy to dwell on—loss, anxiety, guilt, anger, failure, and worst-case scenarios—and focusing instead on past successes, new habits, and best-case scenarios.

In other words, we have it in us to emerge from the darkest tragedies stronger, better, and more capable.

Now that more than two years have passed since the bombing in Ukraine, I have enough perspective to say that the opportunity for growth after trauma is not only very real but also highly attainable. There are practical steps we can take to determine the paths our journeys will take. None of them are easy. Nothing is guaranteed. But it doesn't take superhuman strength to tap into our inner resilience. This remarkable power is already within us, waiting for us to deploy it.

* * *

There are moments in my life now—not many, but one or two—when something happens that just leaves me in awe.

One day when I was working on something in the living room of our new home, Alicia came over and said she had something important to tell me.

"I'm pregnant," she matter-of-factly declared.

In that moment, my life changed forever again.

Back when we started dating, Alicia and I agreed we wanted children, though looking back she thinks I may not have been fully aware of what I was getting into. "I don't think you quite understood what having a baby meant," she once told me. "You were at the delivery, you were always very supportive, and you knew how important the baby was for me. I'm just not sure you felt as deeply about it as I did."

It's true that at the time I was very focused on my work, and perhaps didn't grasp what a deep bond parenthood can bring. Just one day after the birth of our first daughter, Honor, I started my new job with Fox News. It was, by anyone's standard, a quick turnaround back to work. Alicia knew what journalism meant to me, but she also believed that having children would change me, and she was right.

Growing up, Alicia was extremely close to her sisters, Imogen and Skye, and she'd long had a vision of having three children of her own. She remembered how she and her sisters formed a lifelong alliance against the world, drawing strength and comfort from each other to this day, and she wanted our children to have the same sense of friendship and support and being a team. And, somehow, she willed us to have three daughters, and sure enough that's what they've become—a strong, beautiful, mischievous little team.

Now the team will grow.

Alicia and I both wanted a fourth child, for many reasons, but among them was what happened in Ukraine. For me, having another child was an affirmation of life, an expression of continuity, and a celebration of the thing that mattered most to us—family.

But it was also a chance to redress an issue from my past—the long days and weeks I spent away from my family because of my job. "When we had our babies, you always had to get back to work sooner than later," Alicia told me in one of our talks. "That's just the way our lives were structured. But since you've been home, you've done more with Honor, Iris, and Hero than you ever did, simply by being there. Now you'll get to experience that from babyhood, which is so exciting."

Earlier, in our garden conversation, Alicia said that all our lives are stories, and sometimes we need a chapter in our story to come full circle. For me, becoming a father again, after everything that happened to our family on and since March 14, 2022, is bringing a big part of our story full circle. From out of the ashes and darkness of the bombing, there is new life. In journalistic terms, that's a pretty good narrative arc. Personally, it's one of the most joyous developments of my life.

Since learning Alicia was pregnant, I've spent a lot of time contemplating the things I'll tell our new child about what matters in life. Alicia and I have always been honest with the girls, shielding them when they need shielding (such as when I was injured) but also letting them see the world as it is, the good and the bad. We've both imparted lessons whenever we could—about decency, fairness, family, responsibility—and we've emphasized the importance of self-sufficiency and integrity, in terms they could understand. But since we had Hero, our youngest child, our lives have drastically changed. And I've wondered how what we teach our new child will change because of that.

How, then, will I explain the world to him or her? (As of this writing I don't know if we're having a boy or girl—we never find out ahead of time, we like being surprised—so for now I will refer to our future son or daughter as A.)

Well, when they are old enough, I will tell them this:

A, you were born into a beautiful world but a world that is divided. Everywhere, people see things differently, and they break apart into teams, and they begin to view each other as rivals and enemies, and sometimes it seems like there's nothing that can ever bring everyone together.

But, A, I need you to know there *is* something that unites us all, something bigger and more powerful than any issue that divides us. And that is what I call our common moral backbone as human beings. I've traveled all over the world and been in places where the divisions are so deep, they destroy any sense of normal life. I've been to the most dangerous areas on the planet, and I've seen the very bad things that happen when people no longer trust or believe in each other. It's something I hope you never have to see, but it's important that you know it exists.

But it's even more important that you understand these divisions are not the whole story. Because when I've gone to these broken, seemingly doomed places, and witnessed the worst of human nature, I've also seen the very *best* of humanity. I've seen people risking their lives to help complete strangers. Families saving other families from danger and destruction. Villagers relying on each other to get through horrible catastrophes. And I've seen how reaching out to others and building communities and forging bonds through faith and love are the true defining traits of human beings, and not the hatred and divisions and despair that can derail us.

We are all bound by a common moral backbone and a shared will to do what's right and good. That's what your grandfather Roderick taught me when I was your age—that we all instinctively know the right thing to do, and that we must try as hard as we can to always do that thing. Of course, we are human, and humans are fallible, and sometimes people lose their way, and sometimes whole groups of people turn their backs on our shared humanity. But in the end, this common moral backbone is unbreakable. It will always be there. I know this is true, because I've seen how it endures in the most hate-ravaged places on earth. There will never be anything more powerful anywhere than two people talking to each other, finding their commonality, helping each other in hard times and building communities in which they can thrive.

We can rely on this. Our backbone holds up under enormous pressure. It is our true nature as human beings. So, A, don't ever be cynical about the world, and don't ever despair that we can't mend what's broken. Be hopeful, be positive, *believe* in what we can do when we come together. I need you to know this as you grow up and go out into society, because I want you to be a force for good and an agent for positive change. I need you to be strong and determined, and I need you to use that unbreakable backbone to fix the world.

A, one day I will tell you the full story of what happened to me in Ukraine. You've seen my so-called robot leg, and in your innocence, you thought nothing of it. Maybe you thought everyone eventually grows a robot leg. But as you get older, you'll have more questions, and I'll answer them as best I can. I'll tell you why I went to Ukraine, and what the people of that country were going through, and why I put myself in risky situations. Some of it will make sense; some might not. Believe me, I don't have all the answers. But when you get older and we talk about what happened, I hope I can convey to you how beautiful life is, and how it's worth fighting for—but also how terribly fragile it can be.

I won't tell you this to make you fearful. I will say it to impress on you how we should live life to the fullest every moment of every day. How we should never take our lives for granted and instead savor all the things that make life so wonderful. When you're old enough, I'll share the stories of the close calls my colleagues and I had, where survival depended on a few random decisions. I'll tell you about Trey Yingst, my colleague at Fox News, who was in Israel the day of the Hamas attack and headed to the Gaza border to cover the fighting. How by chance his car got stuck behind an ambulance near the border, and how the ten-minute delay stopped them from driving straight into the terrorists and almost surely being kidnapped or worse.

And I'll compare that to my story, and how, when I was in Horenka outside Kyiv shooting a report about the devastated village, my fate was decided by a series of tiny decisions, any one of which, if made differently, could have spared me from my injuries or perhaps made them worse. What if Ukrainian soldiers had allowed us to film them digging trenches, as we'd planned, and hadn't suggested we go to Horenka? What if we'd stayed in the village longer and filmed more spots? What if we'd gone left instead of right? Driven there and not here? What if our car hadn't stalled while we were reversing away from the first missile? These questions are unanswerable, but they illustrate how fragile life can be, particularly in times and places of conflict. I tell you these things because I want you to fully appreciate what a gift life is, in the hopes that you'll treasure every day.

I certainly want to tell you how you won the lottery in the mother department. Your mom, Alicia, has sacrificed so much for me, starting with our sense of privacy at home. You've seen the carers and therapists streaming in and out most days, and they'll likely continue to be part of our lives for a while yet. Between me and you and your sisters and all these people, Alicia is almost never alone in our home. But she is brilliant at adapting to new challenges and situations—she just does whatever needs to be done. Of course, she worries about me, though not as much these days—I'm feeling really healthy and strong, and it doesn't take me an hour and a half to get ready in the morning or go to the store and back. She worries about what will happen when I get older, when we all slow down and get a little creaky. I assure her that I'll be just fine—I'm pretty good at adapting to new situations too—and I tell her that whatever happens, we'll all get through it together.

A, I also want you to know that what happened to me in Ukraine, as gruesome as it may sound, has been a pure blessing. You see, before the bombing I was on a certain path, and sometimes my focus was mostly on my work as a journalist, and as a result I was away from your mother and your sisters and our home for long stretches, and I think in that time I missed many beautiful moments I wish I'd been there to see. A ballet recital. A birthday party. One of your sisters playing with Bosco. Just the funny little moments of daily life. And now, because of what happened to me, I get to spend much more time with you all, and I am there for more of those little moments, and I am *so* grateful for that.

Your mother will tell you the same thing—I've become a much more hands-on father. After the bombing, your mother would drive your two oldest sisters to school and come back home to find me coloring or doing puzzles with their youngest sister, Hero. Neither of us says it, but we both know that's just not something I would have done before my injuries. Now I can't wait to start a new game of backgammon with Honor, who is every bit as competitive as I am, and who I generally beat because I don't believe in always making life easy for your kids, but who I sometimes allow to win to show her it can be done (don't tell her I told you that— and, you know, to be fair, more and more Honor beats me fair and square). And I can't wait to play hide-and-seek with Iris just before bed, marveling at how she keeps finding new places to hide, because Iris is always thinking outside the box, always being creative. A, you and I will have our own game we love playing, and I promise I'll never let you win—unless you give me that puppy-dog look and basically leave me no choice.

I think I will tell you about two very special people who were part of my life—my longtime great friend Pierre Zakrzewski, a Fox News cameraman, and a young Ukrainian journalist named Oleksandra Kuvshynova, or Sasha, who I only knew for a short time. Pierre and Sasha were sitting on either side of me in the back of the small car we drove to Horenka. The missiles struck, and I survived. They didn't. Every day since, I've thought about them and I've missed them, and on some days, I've struggled to understand why they didn't make it and I did. I haven't come up with an answer yet, and I'm not sure there is one. Luck? Fate? The sheer randomness of existence? There's no way to know. And in a way, not knowing has added to the terrible sense of loss I feel when I think about those two brave souls.

You will figure out on your own that everyone faces crushing loss sooner or later—that adversity and sorrow are just part of the deal. The tough times will come, some tougher than others, some seemingly unbearable, and when they come, we must all find ways to get through them somehow. That is also part of the deal. My message to you, then, is that *we cannot allow loss to hold us back*. When I think about Pierre and Sasha, it would be easy for me to crumble under the sadness of losing them, but instead I try very hard to use their passing as motivation. I want them to motivate me to get the very most out of my life to honor them and the sacrifice they made. I know Pierre would not have wanted to see me wallowing in grief and wasting precious days. After a while, he would have wanted me to resume my life with even more vigor, to experience everything fully the way he would have if he were still here. That is the greatest tribute we can pay to those we've lost—to make our lives worthy of the courageous, heroic examples they set.

Do not let life's hardships slow you down. Do not let fear of failure stop you from taking big chances. Do not let any challenge overwhelm you—break them down into little steps and take one tiny step at a time. Do not let the currents sweep you off line: keep kicking, keep going, keep moving forward. Even if you can't see through the clouds and the storm, keep pushing until you can.

Be bold. Be driven. Believe in yourself.

But also, A—please take time to *breathe*.

This is a lesson I thought I'd learned, but that I had to relearn after the bombing. In life, we want to be purposeful and passionate and always driving forward, *but we mustn't let that drive and resolve cause us to miss the simple joys of life*. What I've learned in the many months since I was injured is that the small things matter, and maybe even matter most of all. My life had to slow down considerably for me to realize that the world offers us many tiny moments of absolute joy—moments when we feel truly grateful to be alive—and that it is very, very easy to miss them if we keep our blinders on. I know these lessons may sound contradictory—be driven, never slow down, but also take time to breathe—but really, they're not. Because the moments I'm talking about are like little flashes of light—it hardly takes any time to notice them, and then, just like that, they're gone.

I'll give you an example. Your grandfather, Roderick, loved trees. He loved trees so much he used to carefully plant them wherever he could and take pleasure in imagining how they'd look in fifty or a hundred years, when he'd no longer be around to sit under them.

He got so much joy out of trees, and when I was growing up, I guess I found that a little odd. I mean, trees are trees, right? Trunk, branches, leaves. There's millions of them everywhere. How could someone derive such joy out of that? I didn't get it.

But now—I get it.

After we moved to our new house in London, I was lying in bed one morning when I looked out the window and for the first time noticed a tree on the street outside.

It was a huge white tree with these thick, knuckled branches reaching for the heavens like giant fingers. That morning, the sky was cloudless and bright blue, framing the tree in a way that took my breath away. I marveled at all the details that defined it—the mighty trunk supporting strong branches, all topped by the smallest, most delicate leaves, proudly fluttering. The tree struck me as a miraculous work of art, so perfect, so balanced, yet so unwilling to bend to anything except its unique design. Suddenly I understood why my father loved trees so much, and when I did, I felt a profound connection to him. Surely my father, a man of black-and-white moralism, prized how stalwart trees are, how they grow so steadily despite the ups and downs of life, how they stand for hundreds of years, often unnoticed, rarely appreciated. In that moment, in that fleeting flash of light, I got it—I understood. There is joy for us in the smallest, most ordinary things, just waiting for us to take a breath and notice.

Finally, A, I want you to know that your mother and I both feel incredibly hopeful for the future—for *your* future. For sure it is a challenging time to live in, but if I've learned anything since the bombing, it's that we all have within us the strength, fortitude, and resolve to rise and meet *any* challenge. If you ever end up reading it, that's what this book is all about—how resilience is our default setting, how we're built to survive and persevere, how we're so much more powerful than we give ourselves credit for.

The hard times will come, A. I wish I could protect you from them, but I can't. All I can do is what I'm doing—telling you what I've learned about resilience, and the ways to activate it, and the need to trust it, and all the steps you can take to empower yourself in times of crisis.

You have it in you. We all do. It's just who we are.

AUTHOR'S NOTE

At 1:15 p.m. on September 6, 2024, Alicia and I welcomed our fourth daughter, Sage, into the world. She is a happy, healthy baby with a shock of dark hair and we're madly in love with her.

The moment I held Sage for the first time I felt profound joy and wonder. I thought of how the immense power of a life beginning co-exists with the great sorrow of losing loved ones, in the vast, beautiful cycle of existence.

And in that moment, after everything we've experienced as a family in the last three years, I understood that nothing in the world could ever matter more than this precious little life I held in my hands.

ACKNOWLEDGMENTS

Before all else, I need to thank my wonderful family—my beautiful wife, Alicia, who is always there for me no matter what and makes me better in every way, and our lovely daughters Honor, Iris, Hero, and Sage, without whom I simply wouldn't be here.

Thank you to my parents, Roderick and Jenny Hall, for teaching me right and wrong and giving me the will to live an adventurous life. To Aunt Connie, who leads us all, and to my brothers, Barnaby, Andrew, Peter, and Michael, and my sister, Nonie.

Thank you to the Mellers and Lukins—Kim, Scarlett, Imogen, Chris, and Skye. I am so honored to be part of your family and to get to grow alongside you all.

A special thank-you to Olivia Metzger, who is firstly the kindest and warmest friend and part of my family, and secondly my brilliant agent. You have guided and supported us, cared for us, and you dream big for all of us too.

My deepest thanks to the tireless Sarah Verardo and everyone at Save Our Allies, for being the superheroes the world needs right now—and for literally saving my life.

Thank you to my great friend Pierre Zakrzewski—you are with me everywhere I go, always pushing me to live bigger. You helped make the world a smaller, better place. And to Oleksandra Kuvshynova—Sasha, your uncommon bravery and sacrifice will never be forgotten.

A very heartfelt thank-you to all my fellow war correspondents everywhere, who, like Pierre and Sasha, take enormous risks to shine a light on the truth and lay bare the world's evils. My respect for you is boundless.

Thank you to the U.S. military, the greatest force for justice history has ever known. Many decades ago, it was a squad of U.S. soldiers who saved my father's life during World War II, and in 2022, it was U.S. soldiers yet again who saved mine. There is no way I can thank you all enough for your service and sacrifice, other than by living with purpose and resolve in your honor.

Thank you, deeply and sincerely, to my great team at Fox News. To Lachlan and the Murdoch family—you have helped and encouraged me from the very minute this happened; thank you for caring so deeply about journalism and journalists, and everyone who works at Fox. To Suzanne Scott—you've offered nonstop support to me and my family, and you have allowed me to continue doing what I love. To Jay Wallace—you've encouraged me through this ordeal, and you've never stopped checking in, and I'm proud to have you as a friend. To Greg Headen—it feels like we've become old friends, and for you I'll sign a thousand books. To Lauren Peterson and Kim Rosenberg, two of the most creative and kindest people in the business. To Dragan Petrovic—you've been there since my very first day at Fox, and you will forever be family to me. To Trey Yingst— you remind me of me and I'm immensely proud of everything you do. To everyone at the London bureau—that's where it all began, and it's always felt like home; thank you for making it feel that way.

To everyone in the New York and DC bureaus—when I think of a newsroom, I know that you are exactly what a newsroom should be; you're all the hardest-working and closest team in the business, and I wish you all the best of the best. To Irena and Caley—you've been there as great guides throughout, and I'm grateful for that. To Dudi Gamliel—you will always be *the man*. To Yael Rotem Kuriel, and all the Israel team—you never stop looking for stories, and you inspire me. To Kaitlyn and Kiara—you are the best podcast producers I could ever have asked for, and you've built our little thing into something very special; thank you to Jason and John for guiding the podcast and helping it grow. To Jason Klarman, thank you for supporting me at Fox Nation, and for your support overall. To Maryam—your creativity and meticulousness have led the way for me.

To the U.S. Secretary of State Antony Blinken, thank you—you called me soon after the bombing in Ukraine and inspired me more than you'll ever know. Thank you for sharing your time and uncanny wisdom with me.

A very special thank you to my magical team at HarperCollins—to Lisa Sharkey, the brains, heart, and guts behind it all; to my wonderful editor, Maddie Pillari, for a series of crucial insights and suggestions; to editorial assistant Lexie von Zedlitz and to the art director, copyeditors, and everyone else at Harper who poured their special excellence into this project.

Thank you to Tom Croft and Ashley for helping my family create our new home, and to Phill Gill—who understood what many others didn't.

Thank you to Helen, Sam, Dave, and Jack and everyone at Remedy—you make my life, and so many other lives, so much better.

To Jamie, Nicole, and all at Pace—thank you for getting me up and walking!

Thank you to Andrea, someone in whom I have total and utter trust.

Thank you to Lor, you are family to us all, and to Bella, for all you do for to help us.

Thank you deeply to Dr. Shehan Hettiaratchy and Dr. Brian Mac-Greevy, my two remarkable London doctors—where would I be without your brilliance?

Thank you from the bottom of my heart to everyone at the Brooke Army Medical Center, or BAMC—you all picked me up when I was torn apart and put me back together. And a special word for John Ferguson—you saved so many people and you are dearly missed by us all. You left an indelible mark on the world.

Thank you to my case manager Jason Chidwick—all of this would have been so much harder without you. Thank you for taking away the tough parts.

Thank you to James (Blue Beard)—you were an inspiration to me at BAMC, and you are an inspiration to me now.

Thank you to Pete, for keeping me looking young, and for being one of the most open and honest people I know.

Thank you to all my brilliant friends of whom there are too many to name—please know you mean much more to me than I can put in words.

I want to offer a special word of praise, affection, and hope for the people of Ukraine, both soldiers and civilians—your unfathomable strength and resiliency is changing and inspiring the entire world. I am in awe of you.

And finally, my heartiest thank you to all of you out there who have followed my story and offered me your kindness and support.

I need you to know that all of your concern and well wishes have been nothing short of crucial for me in my recovery, and I can only hope that sharing my story with you has somehow resonated in your lives. If I can do what I did, you all can do whatever you set your minds to.

ABOUT THE AUTHOR

BENJAMIN HALL joined Fox News Channel in 2015. A longtime war correspondent who has covered conflicts around the world, he has written for the *New York Times*, the *Sunday Times*, the BBC, the *Times* (London), Agence France-Presse, the *Independent*, and *Esquire*. His first book about Ukraine, *Saved*, was published in 2023. Ben lives with his wife and their four children in London.